THE FOREST BEFORE THE FIELD

A Guide for Pioneers

Melody Farrell

THIS BOOK IS PUBLISHED BY LOST POET PRESS

Published in the United States by Lost Poet Press.

First Paperback edition.

www.lostpoetpress.com

www.pioneercircle.org

www.circleacamp.com

ISBN 978-1-944470-20-3

For my dad, the best storyteller I’ve ever known.

Table of Contents

Prologue

Welcome to the Woods

The woods are lovely, dark and deep.
But I have promises to keep,
And miles to go before I sleep,
And miles to go before I sleep.

Robert Frost

It seems we have found ourselves together amid this cold, dark forest. I am delighted to meet you. These woods can be quite lonely, as you have learned by now. Come, warm yourself by the fire for a moment. Let us talk of what brought you here, and of what will draw you onward. By the light of the fire, we shall find some warmth, some illumination, and some good company.

Perhaps you are surprised to find me here, for I am not so young as you are. On the other hand, I am not surprised to find you. In fact, I have been waiting for you, praying for the day you would arrive. I have been preparing for your visit, hoping that I just might have a chance to meet you as you pass this way.

You see, we need you here. This forest is not just any forest. *It is the forest before the field.*

What is this field, you ask? Wise questions already, Young Traveler. But not so fast. We have much to discuss this night by the fire, much to consider before we talk about the field that lies ahead.

First, let us talk about what brought you here, to this very forest, on this very day. The only way one finds themselves in this forest is by having a *particular* sort of knowledge. The knowledge comes in diverse ways and at various times. Sometimes it screams, but mostly it whispers. You have discovered this knowledge, whether someone has sent you to this forest or whether you have found your way here all alone. One way or another you have heard the truth: *all is not as it should be*. All is not as it is *meant* to be.

If you have found your way to this forest, then you already know the world is not meant to be such a cold and dark place. There is something in you that knows the warm beauty that once filled our world has slowly faded into a cold, dreary, dullness. There is something in you that believes you are meant to be a light, meant to reveal a beauty that has been forgotten.

If you have found your way to this forest, you might also already know that the stories you have been told are *not all true*. Indeed, you have seen evidence that the stories this world is building itself upon may be crumbling at their very foundation, and you may be wondering what is to become of a world without a story.

Ah, but there is something enchanted about this fire, Young Traveler.

By this fire, we can remember the True Story that the world has all but forgotten.

I may not have the answers you seek for your journey ahead, but I do have some stories that can serve as your guide. I have labored for many years to read and seek and tell and live the stories that are true. If you allow me, I will share them with you as we sit by this fire together. Some may be tales that you already know, and I pray they will serve to remind you of the True Story.

There may be fearsome things to face on the other side of these woods, Young Traveler. You are going to need every True Story you can find if you are going to navigate your way ahead.

Before you leave this fire, you will have to make a choice.

Will you journey ahead, beyond the forest and into the field? It is not as simple a choice as you may suppose. There are other paths you could take, and there are other voices who will call to you.

There are factions to the east, willing you to turn away, to distract yourself with the pleasures and indulgences of a world in excess. You will hear the loud voices of the entertainers and the merchants, hoping you will come to consume every diversion they have to offer and thereby forget the troubles of a world without a True Story. They will tell you that nothing really matters except your own satisfaction, and if you are not careful, they may convince you that they are right.

There are factions to the west, calling you to work hard and long, to produce increasingly as you rise to the pinnacle of human achievement. You will hear the judgmental voices of the establishments and institutions, shaming you for your lack of production and coercing you to prove your worth to the world. They will tell you that you will never matter unless you earn your way to significance, and if you are not careful, they may enslave you to their selfish greed.

There are factions from behind, bidding you back from this forest, back to the familiar facades of the false stories. They may think they are keeping you safe by attempting to hold you away from the field ahead, hoping that other pioneers will blaze a trail so that you can simply follow. While they mean well, they are driven by fear, and fear is neither a kind master nor a wise teacher. If you are not careful, they may frighten you away from the great adventure that awaits you.

And we cannot forget there are also factions from the darkness, from the world beyond the scope of our sight, enticing you to forget the light in the first place. These voices would have you believe that there is no world beyond this world, there is no God, there is no story, and there is no hope. They will tell you that despair and desolation are the anthems of your age, and if you are not careful, they will lead you to your doom.

But, Young Traveler, these voices are nothing to fear, for these voices have no power over you unless you give that power to them.

Here, by the light of the fire, amid the forest, let me speak the truth to you.

You are a pioneer.

Pioneers are not confused by voices who would draw them away from the path they are meant to pursue.

Pioneers move forward with wisdom and purpose, blazing a trail for all to follow.

Pioneers begin with imagination, endure through determination, and finish with courage.

How do I know you are a pioneer?

You can sense the change in the wind, aiming you ahead into the great unknown.

You can hear the sounds in the forest, calling you to come onward into the great mystery of your becoming.

You can see the light that still shines, compelling you by beauty, for beauty.

You can feel the pull of the True Story, drawing you away from the false stories and into the hope of a narrative that will one day end as all great stories end.

In peace. In love. In redemption.

Ah yes, I sense the stirrings in your heart, an awareness that there is a truth to my words. So let us share some stories together. I will tell you some true stories about the world, and some true things about you. When we have finished our chat by the fire, perhaps you will be ready to make your path through the forest all the way to the field.

Chapter One

A Story of Love

Stories are light.
Light is precious in a world so dark.
Begin at the beginning.
Tell ... a story.
Make some light.

Kate DiCamillo

Once upon a time there lived a king and queen who gave birth to a beautiful baby girl. The child was beloved across the land from the moment of her arrival, and the king and queen celebrated her coming with feasting and extraordinary joy.

When the girl was just eight years old, an evil sorcerer snuck into the palace, killed the queen, and stole the child away. He locked her in the dank dungeon of his fortress, her only company the sorcerer himself, who came daily to feed her and mock her. He cast a spell over her, a spell that made her forget who she was and where she came from. The evil sorcerer kept the princess caged in her cell, and each day he would whisper the same message to her as he passed her food.

"Filthy child... ugly child... wretched child. You are too feeble to clean the floors of this fortress. In the dungeon you'll stay, until you rot away!"

The girl grew up with the recurring message playing in her ears and head and her heart. Feeling vile and worthless, she sat day after day, year after year, with nothing to do but count the bricks in her cell and wonder where she had come from and who she was. Though the spell of the sorcerer was strong, and his words were cruel, there was something inside the princess that never quite believed him.

There was something in the princess that believed she was worth something to someone.

Four years passed, and finally the king and all his armies broke through the enchantments surrounding the fortress, vanquished the evil sorcerer, and rescued the princess from the dungeon that had become her home.

The girl was confused and afraid as the carriage took her back to the safety of her father's castle. She could remember nothing of her family or her home. All she could remember were the curses of the sorcerer. No one had told her who she was, but if they had, she would never have believed them.

A kind woman brought her into the palace and tucked her into a massive bed with the softest sheets and the fluffiest pillows. The princess fell asleep in the warmth and luxury of the home that should have always been hers, but when she awoke in the morning, a sense of dread filled her.

"I am filthy! I am ugly! I am worthless! I am not fit to sleep in this bed, not fit even to clean the floors of this palace! I must run away! I must discover who I really am and who I am meant to become!"

The princess waited at her door until the hallway was empty. She escaped the palace and made it out onto the streets of the city, determined to uncover her identity.

She came first to a stable nearby. A groomsman was polishing a saddle as she approached, and she looked at him hopefully.

"Please, sir, might I have a job at your fine stables? I could sweep the floor, or polish the saddles, or groom the horses?"

The groomsman, not recognizing her as the princess, agreed to give her a chance. She labored as hard as she could, but it quickly became clear that she had no knack for working in the stables. Her hands were unaccustomed to the sweeping, and they became bloodied by the repeated motions. Her arms were not strong enough to polish the saddles, and they did not glisten as they were meant to. Her heart was not calm around the horses, and they jumped away from her touch.

"I'm sorry, lass," the groomsman said. "It does not appear you were born to be a stable hand."

The princess sadly made her way out of the stables and down the street until she came to a bakery.

"Please, ma'am," she said urgently to the woman baking bread inside. "Are you looking for some kitchen help? I could work for you, wash your dishes, clean your countertops."

The baker, not recognizing her as the princess, agreed to give her a chance. The girl worked furiously, but it soon became clear that she had no gift for working in the kitchen. She was not tall enough to reach the dishes in the bottom of the sink, her shoes tracked in mud from the stables, and as she was wiping the countertop, she burned her hand on a pan fresh from the oven.

"There, there, dear," said the baker as she wiped the girl's tears. "Not everyone is born to be a baker. This just is not the place for you."

Defeated, the princess looked back at the castle she had come from. It felt familiar, somehow. It felt compelling. There must be a job inside where she could earn her keep. She made her way back inside and found a maid cleaning on the stairs.

"Please ma'am," she said hopefully. "Could you teach me how to be a maid in this castle? I could help you with your work for the day?"

"Certainly not!" the maid replied crossly, not recognizing her as the princess. "Just look at you! You are a mess! You have got food on your dress, dirt on your shoes, and your hair is a veritable disaster. You are clearly not born to clean in a castle!"

"No, she is not," boomed a voice from the foyer below. "She will do no cleaning here."

Filthy child. Ugly child. Vile child. The taunts of the sorcerer played in her ears.

"Your majesty!" the maid exclaimed, bowing low in reverence to the king.

"Come here, my dear," he called to the princess.

She turned to look, taking in the sight of the king, who stood gazing at her with the strangest expression she had ever seen. She followed the sound of his voice without delay, heeding his call to come. As she walked closer, all the hair on her arms and neck stood on end. It was not because she was in the presence of royalty... it was because as she gazed at the king, she realized that it was like looking in a mirror. He had the same curly hair, the same green eyes, the same pale skin, the same stubborn tilt to his jaw.

Without a word passing between them, and without a thought

of her bedraggled appearance, she flung herself into his arms. She knew who she was, for the enchantment was broken.

She was a child of the king, and she was born to become like him.

The False Story

If you live in the world of the modern age, you have heard a false story more times than you can count: **You must prove that you are worthy of love.**

Not only have you heard this story, but you have lived it. Your grades and good behavior win you the approval of your teachers. Your athletic skills or personal charm win you popularity in your school. Your performance and production win you promotions in your job. Your looks, possessions, and charisma win you more options for romance. And through it all, you find yourself wondering who it is you are supposed to be, and what it is that you are supposed to be becoming.

Some relationships in your life may be built around something truer, but some are not. You are left thinking that life is one big proving ground whereby you must tirelessly, endlessly, painfully achieve the right to be loved. Eventually, you fear you will become not the person you are created to be, but rather the person who can win the most approval and earn the most love.

This, Young Traveler, is a false story. Let me tell you what is true.

The True Story

If you hear nothing else I say to you while we sit here by the fire, hear this: **You are loved**. The God who created you, loves you. You are worthy of love simply because you are His creation. You are worthy of joy, happiness, and blessing because He has called you blessed. There is nothing you must do to prove your worth, nothing you can do to earn His love, because He has already given it to you.

My father quoted these wise words more times than I can count, but they make my heart well up with gratitude every time I hear them: "What you have been working so hard to get, *you've already got* – a self worth loving."

In our story, the princess knew, deep down, that she belonged to someone. She knew, deep down, that she was worth something, and that she had an identity. And yet, the enchantment upon her was strong. If she had not encountered her father and seen her reflection in his face, she may never have known the love he felt for her or the story she was born to live in.

Her story is our story, dear ones. And if we are to leave this forest and pioneer our way through the field, we cannot properly do so without a foundational knowledge of who we are.

It will serve you well to refer to the ancient text of wisdom and truth if you are to live in the True Story. The apostle John, a pioneer of his time, penned these words:

1 John 3:1-3 NLT

> *See how very much our Father loves us, for he calls us his children, and that is what we are! But the people who belong to this world don't recognize that we are God's children because they don't know him. Dear friends, we are already God's children, but he has not yet shown us what we will be like when Christ appears. But we do know that we will be like him, for we will see him as he really is.*

There is a mystery to uncover here, in this love of a Creator. A mystery that this world cannot fully understand, or fully recognize. There are pieces of the story we do not understand yet, for the end of the story has not come. But as we pioneer our way forward, from the forest to the field, we must do so without forgetting the very nature of who we are, and the deep love that we already receive from the God who is the author of the True Story.

Kings and Queens, Wizards and Jedi

There are many stories that have been told about Young Travelers such as yourself who discover who they truly are. In fact, most of the great stories include this narrative, because most of the great stories point us back to the True Story.

Take, for instance, the adventures of Peter, Susan, Edmund, and Lucy in the classic tale from C.S. Lewis, *The Lion, The Witch, and the Wardrobe*. The children find themselves carried away to a magical land, where they must restore life and beauty to a world turned cold and taken over by evil. In the story, the children were already meant to become the kings and queens of Narnia, long before they were ever born. After they assist the great lion Aslan in his defeat of the White Witch, they reign on the thrones of Cair Paravel, thrones made specifically for them.

The first time the children hear the name, Aslan (who is the representation of Jesus in the story), this is what happens:

> *"None of the children knew who Aslan was any more than you do; but the moment the Beaver had spoken these words everyone felt quite different. Perhaps it has sometimes happened to you in a dream that someone says something which you don't understand but in the dream it feels as if it had some enormous meaning--either a terrifying one which turns the whole dream into a nightmare or else a lovely meaning too lovely to put into words, which makes the dream so beautiful that you remember it all your life and are always wishing you could get into that dream again. It was like that now. At the name of Aslan each one of the children felt*

> *something jump in its inside. Edmund felt a sensation of mysterious horror. Peter felt suddenly brave and adventurous. Susan felt as if some delicious smell or some delightful strain of music had just floated by her. And Lucy got the feeling you have when you wake up in the morning and realize that it is the beginning of the holidays or the beginning of summer."* [1]

Perhaps what the children felt on this day is the same sort of feeling you are beginning to have as you sit here around this fire. You see, Aslan exists in our world too, only here, we call him Jesus. And just as the children were born into the human world but meant to be Kings and Queens of Narnia, so too were you born into the human world but meant to be Sons and Daughters of God.

Another story you may be familiar with is the tale of a young Harry Potter. A magical letter calls this child away to wizarding school, though he has no idea he is a wizard. Through the many twists and turns of his story, we discover that there is something particularly important about the magic within him, something that was created because of the *love of his parents.* He goes on to use this magic to defeat the evil that threatens his world.

We could also tell the story of young Luke Skywalker, hidden away on Tatooine and unaware of the great power within him. Through his adventures, he discovers that not only does the galaxy need him to defeat the darkness, but that he was born to do so. While the love of his father is not evident until the end of his story, there remain echoes of the one True Story.

I could go on to recount dozens of stories, hundreds of stories, about young pioneers who discover their true identities. The great storytellers go on telling these great stories because they echo the True Story.

Lost and Found

The story of the princess and her father may remind you of a story from the ancient scriptures.

This is a story that Jesus himself told as a parable to illustrate the love of God for his sons and daughters:

Luke 15:11-24 NLT

> *To illustrate the point further, Jesus told them this story: "A man had two sons. The younger son told his father, 'I want my share of your estate now before you die.' So his father agreed to divide his wealth between his sons.*
>
> *"A few days later this younger son packed all his belongings and moved to a distant land, and there he wasted all his money in wild living. About the time his money ran out, a great famine swept over the land, and he began to starve. He persuaded a local farmer to*

hire him, and the man sent him into his fields to feed the pigs. The young man became so hungry that even the pods he was feeding the pigs looked good to him. But no one gave him anything.

"When he finally came to his senses, he said to himself, 'At home even the hired servants have food enough to spare, and here I am dying of hunger! I will go home to my father and say, "Father, I have sinned against both heaven and you, and I am no longer worthy of being called your son. Please take me on as a hired servant."'

"So he returned home to his father. And while he was still a long way off, his father saw him coming. Filled with love and compassion, he ran to his son, embraced him, and kissed him. His son said to him, 'Father, I have sinned against both heaven and you, and I am no longer worthy of being called your son.'

"But his father said to the servants, 'Quick! Bring the finest robe in the house and put it on him. Get a ring for his finger and sandals for his feet. And kill the calf we have been fattening. We must celebrate with a feast, for this son of mine was dead and has now returned to life. He was lost, but now he is found.'

Think about those words for a moment: "while he was still a long way off, his father saw him coming. Filled with love and compassion, he ran to his son..."

You see, Young Traveler, the Father is running to you. He longs to embrace you, to welcome you home, to celebrate your return to Love Itself.

The Stories You Will Tell

As you depart from this forest and cut your path through the field, I pray you choose to tell the stories of the children of God.

May this final scripture guide you on your journey.

2 Corinthians 3:16 – 18 NLT

> *But whenever someone turns to the Lord, the veil is taken away. For the Lord is the Spirit, and wherever the Spirit of the Lord is, there is freedom. So all of us who have had that veil removed can see and reflect the glory of the Lord. And the Lord—who is the Spirit—makes us more and more like him as we are changed into his glorious image.*

May you tell tales about our true nature and purpose as sons and daughters of God.

May you love well because the Father first loved you.

May you live a life filled with joy and happiness, flowing from the knowledge that you are beloved.

May you live a life free of fear and worry, free from comparison and competition, free from striving and straining to prove yourself worthy.

May you run freely forward in the knowledge that nothing can separate you from the love of God, and may that knowledge compel you to become his love to others.

Always remember: YOU ARE LOVED. YOU ARE BECOMING LOVE. YOU ARE A PIONEER.

Glass Box

Thought I was free
I thought that I could run away
I thought I found
Escape from being on display
I tried to go
I found these walls I can't move past
And now I'm stuck
And they are laughing through the glass

Dance little one in your glass box
Dance to the rhythm of whoever knocks
Don't you dare to stop 'til you collapse
Then lay there flat, barely catch your breath
Now up again - you can't refuse
Don't even pretend like you get to choose
You are just a puppet in a prison now
So smile and act and dance and dance and dance

Now is this true?
Is this the life I'm meant to live?
Alone and forced
To offer more than I can give?
It won't shut up,
This voice that's screaming in my ear
It can't be right
And yet this is all I hear:

Dance little one in your glass box
Dance to the rhythm of whoever knocks
Don't you dare to stop 'til you collapse
Then lay there flat, barely catch your breath
Now up again - you can't refuse
Don't even pretend like you get to choose
You are just a puppet in a prison now

So smile and act and dance and dance and dance

These lies will tell my story if I let them
This pain defines my world
If I give an inch of ground
These screams have become so loud,
And yet I can't forget
That once I heard another sound...

The sound of truth
Echoes in the quiet
The song of love
I can almost hear it
A breath of hope
Rising up
against the LIE

Dance little one cause you are free
Dance to the rhythm that's in step with Me
You won't need to stop, I'll give you breath
You won't want to stop, I'll hold your hand
Together now, cause I chose you
And waited for the day you'd choose me too
The glass is gone, so come, my love
We'll smile and laugh and dance and dance and dance

Chapter Two

A Story of Enchantment

There are no ordinary people.
You have never talked to a mere mortal.

C.S. Lewis

Once there was an artist, a painter by trade. He lived in a little cottage atop a hill. Every day he would wake before dawn, overflowing with enough inspiration to craft a hundred paintings. As early as he could each day, he set to work with his paints at his easel, masterfully creating the pictures that he would take to town and to the great cities nearby. Though he lived as a humble painter, his work was known throughout the land where he was respected as a great master.

The artist had a son, a young boy. The artist loved his son dearly, and lavished love upon the boy in every way a father should. Much of the inspiration for his art came from the love he had for his son, and the artist was filled with joy every time he looked at the young boy.

The painter knew that one day his son would want to become an artist, too.

The boy took an interest in the artist's work. He would watch his father lay out the paints each morning, paying careful attention to how the brush met the canvas and how the strokes of his father's hands affected the lines and shapes that he created. Sometimes the boy would mimic his father's movements or touch his father's brushes, and the artist's heart filled with anticipation of all that his son could become.

The day came when it was time for the boy to create his first work of art. The son had watched his father long enough to know how to lay out the paints, how to prepare the brushes and the canvas and the easel for the work. The father watched, his heart filled with joy and wonder as his son began to create.

"What are you going to paint?" the artist asked.

"The grass, and trees ... the sun and flowers," the boy said simply, focused on the palette before him.

"Ah, a landscape! How wonderful!" the artist encouraged.

He watched with rapt attention as the boy began. The strokes were stiff, and the paint was sloppy, but the boy went after the piece of art with passion and enthusiasm, and the artist was delighted.

And yet, the father knew something would hinder his young son from a full expression of his craft, at least for a while.

"Son ... I see the trees you have made here ... the grass, the sun. I can make out the shapes – well done, my boy! But ... can you tell me ... why have you made the grass purple, and the sun blue?"

The boy stared for a moment at the painting.

"What do you mean ... purple? What is blue?"

The artist grew quiet for a moment as he gathered the compassion to share the truth with his son.

"The colors ... you cannot see the colors, my boy."

"What ... what are colors?"

The artist sat to look the boy gently in the eyes and tell him the sorrowful news: he was colorblind.

The father felt a deep ache, for he knew that he would not be able to fully share in the joy of creation with his son. They would speak different languages. His son would never see the full scope of beauty that the father longed to create just for him.

But the father loved his son. And even if the boy could never fully appreciate the art, or the creations of the father, that would not and could not change the love he had for his son.

In the months and years to come, the father never stopped trying to share his love for art with his son. The great chasm between them, the chasm between what his son could see and what his son could not see, never stopped them from trying to connect. One day, the boy asked his father to try and teach him the colors.

"If you show me" the boy said, "which is the color of grass, then I will paint my grass like you. If you show me which colors make up the sky, I will try and blend them like you do. If you show me which color the sun is, then maybe one day I could make a sun that would shine like yours does."

The artist's eyes filled with tears of joy. Even though his son could not understand what he was asking, even though he could never see the full beauty of what he was creating ... the boy wanted to learn.

And so, the artist taught. Every day he showed the boy what colors to use. He stood beside the easel every single time the boy came to paint, guiding his brush to the colors that would bring the most beauty to the canvas before them. He never left the boy's side, never stopped guiding his brush and encouraging his art.

Soon, their work became known throughout the land. It was not the same work as his father, but it was still beautiful, and valuable, and good. Better, in some ways, than when the artist had painted on his own.

The boy enjoyed his work and his art, but always with a sense of longing. Always with a feeling that he could never fully please his father, or never fully know his father, because he could never see as his father saw.

And then one day, everything changed.

A large, black raven approached the little cottage on the hill. The artist saw her approaching and knew that this raven was no ordinary bird. He rushed outside to intercept her before she could speak to his son.

"What business do you have here?" the artist asked.

"Only the business that you would find most valuable, oh master artist," the raven said with a shrill, haunting sort of voice.

"And what is that?" he asked warily.

"I know the curse upon your son," she whispered. "I cast it myself, and I can reverse it, if you wish."

The raven offered the artist a trade. She would release her magical enchantment upon the boy, allowing the father to buy back full vision with all the range and scope and depth of color for his son ... and all it would cost him was his own sight.

The artist agreed before the raven had even finished talking. He had settled in his heart long ago that if ever there were a way, magic or otherwise, to buy back the gift of color for his son, he would pay any price for it.

The moment that the father agreed, the raven flew at the man and ripped his eyes from their very sockets, leaving him bleeding upon the ground.

Moments later, the boy ran out of the house, screaming with delight and then with horror, for he had received the gift that the raven promised ... and then he had seen the price that his father had paid to purchase it.

The father did not scream with horror, nor with pain, for all he hoped for had come to pass. His son could see the beauty of the world about him, and more importantly, his son could see the beauty that they had created together.

They walked into the house, a blind artist, and his newly sighted son. And as the son entered the studio where they had spent their lives together creating, the sight stole the very breath from his lungs. There were no words that could be formed to convey the depth of beauty that the boy perceived.

"This," the boy whispered as he looked at the intricate colors upon the canvas. "This is what you've wanted me to see all along."

"Yes," the father laughed. "This is what we have made together! Now, my son ... now you can see it. Now ... everything is new, isn't it?"

The son grew sad again as he looked at his father. "But you?" he asked. "Now you can see nothing?"

The father smiled a deep, satisfied smile.

"I see everything," said the father. "The raven only knows the magic of the darkness. But that is not the only magic that lives here."

The father closed his eyelids, and when they opened again, healthy eyes peered out lovingly, gratefully, joyfully, at his son.

The False Story

You have heard the rumors of this false story before: **The world you can see is the only world there is.**

This is the story that has served to crumble our modern world most deftly. We have convinced ourselves that science and reason are the only gods we need, and when the pursuit of those gods grew old and boring, we simply chose to make ourselves gods. The story of our current age is a story of *humanism*, a story which tells us that humans are the highest good in this world, and that divine beings were never a true part of the story in the first place. A humanist philosophy believes that we can inherently be good enough and virtuous enough and powerful enough to shape our own destinies.

You have heard this story, and if the only ways of discerning truth were the eyes on your face, you may have believed it. Whatever magic and enchantment there is in this world, we rarely perceive it enough to prove it with our physical senses. Whatever Spirit of God moves among us, it does not move often in the visible realm. Whatever evil draws us into darkness, we never see its true form, only the consequences of its presence. Like the boy in the story, we are color blind, unable to see the depth of magic and meaning all around us.

And so, it may be easy to believe that human beings and the world we can see are the only things that exist. It is the way of our modern world. And when we tire of that narrative, and reach the limit of ourselves as gods, it is likely the next false story will involve the virtual gods we create. In the age to come, the world will meld our visible realm with an artificial reality, an "unseen" world that we acknowledge because *we* made it. This is known as *transhumanism*, and it likely awaits you in the field ahead.

All of this, dear one, is a false story. Let me tell you what is true.

The True Story

The boy in the story experienced life as we sometimes do. In a color-blind state, we journey through the days and weeks and years of our lives, frequently oblivious to a world we cannot see. And yet, our Father longs for our wholeness. Our Father created us for relationship with him, for communion and joy as we partake in the beauty of the visible and invisible world.

Here is the True Story: **Every human participates in the enchantment of a seen and unseen reality.**

Now, what do I mean when I say "enchantment"? Is there an actual *magic* to our world?

Well, of course there is, Young Traveler. If you attune yourself to it, you will begin to see the evidence of it, in the captivating sparkle of the sunlight hitting the ocean, or in the graceful and powerful movements of a flock of birds in the sky, or in the grandeur of a mighty mountain. You may begin to taste it, in the sweet, delectable flavor of a fruit grown with care. You may begin to smell it, in the fresh, crisp scent of the forest. You may begin to hear it, in the sounds of a choir singing in perfect harmony. You may begin to feel it, in the embrace of a person you love, or in the warmth of the sun upon your skin.

Yes, there is magic in our world, and we are meant to sense it. This magic serves to remind us of the one True Story, and it serves to create within us a longing for the completion of that story, for the day when all things are restored to wholeness and all things are made new.

C.S. Lewis puts it like this:

> *"If we find ourselves with a desire that nothing in this world can satisfy, the most probable explanation is that we were made for another world."*[2]

We are designed for the world beyond this world, the world of the redeemed, healed, restored version of creation. Like the father and son in the story, we are fashioned to create together, unhindered by our colorblindness and overcome with joy.

But until then, Young Traveler, we make our lives here. And here, in this world, magic is less apparent to our senses.

The World at War

It is not only the magic of the light to which I refer.

The unseen world is a world at war.

We must also attune our senses to the magic of the darkness.

Have you felt the prickle of an evil presence, inciting you to think thoughts of hate, selfishness, or violence? Have you heard a voice of shame, taunting you for your failures and exploiting your insecurities? Have you seen the evidence of abuse, greed, and injustice as it marginalizes the weak and weary of this world?

Of course, you have, for the unseen forces of darkness are hard at work to destroy all that is good, beautiful, and sacred.

But let me warn you of this: the dark magic of the unseen world is much harder to perceive than the magic of the light. This is because the evil in our world does not have to convince us to commit our lives to its service. The evil in this world has only to convince of one thing:

There is no war.

There is no unseen reality. There is no magic. There is only humanity, on a planet that spins around the sun, in a universe that has no creator. And so, the false story perpetuates. Humanism is a great and terrible victory for the darkness, for humans who have made themselves into gods will surely fall into ruin.

Muggles and Marshwiggles

Of all the themes in all the stories told, the stories of enchantment are surely the most plentiful. Why is it, I wonder, that such a vast percentage of classic fairy tales and the ancient myths and the modern classics all tell stories of magic, divine beings, and enchantment?

Ah, but you have caught me there, Young Traveler. I do not wonder why at all.

The reason these stories include the fantastic and mystical is because the fantastic and mystical realm does indeed exist, though just beyond the scope of our sight.

Like the muggles in the stories of Harry Potter, we cannot see or access the magic, at least not most of the time. But our remembrance of its reality has a profound effect on the way we live.

My favorite allegory for the enchanted world comes from another tale in the Narnia series, *The Silver Chair*. In the story, two human children and a Marshwiggle named Puddleglum find themselves on a grand adventure. (If you do not know what a Marshwiggle is, I cannot take the time to explain it to you here, but I quite recommend reading the book to find out.) Near the end of their journey, the travelers are captured and trapped in Underland. In this world, which is a world beneath the world of Narnia, the enchantment forced them to forget that another world exists.

The longer the children and Puddleglum remain in Underland, the more they forget the Narnia they once knew. An evil queen tries to convince them Narnia has never existed, and that they have only imagined it. Puddleglum, the very bravest and best Marshwiggle, resists her sorcery with his whole heart. Even though Narnia has become invisible to his sight and clouded in his memory, he refuses to let the truth be taken from him:

> *"Suppose we have only dreamed, or made up, all those things - trees and grass and sun and moon and stars and Aslan himself. Suppose we have. Then all I can say is that, in that case, the made-up things seem a good deal more important than the real ones. Suppose this black pit of a kingdom of yours is the only world. Well, it strikes me as a pretty poor one. And that's a funny thing, when you come to think of it. We're just babies making up a game, if you're right. But four babies playing a game can make a play-world which licks your real world hollow. That's why I'm going to stand by the play world. I'm on Aslan's side even if there isn't any Aslan to lead it. I'm going to live as like a Narnian as I can even if there isn't any Narnia."*[3]

And so, like Puddleglum, may we fight for the memories and mysteries of the enchanted realm. May we live like children of the King, even when we cannot perceive him with our eyes. May we love like Jesus did, even though we cannot touch him with our hands.

At the beginning of the epic three-part *Lord of the Rings* movie trilogy, there is a prologue voiced over by Lady Galadriel. This is what she says:

"The world is changed.

I feel it in the water.

I feel it in the earth.

I smell it in the air.

Much that once was is lost, for none now live who remember it."[4]

As you pioneer your way from the forest to the field, **may you live to be one who remembers.**

The Enchantment Within You

May we never forget this part of the True Story: there is not only an enchantment that surrounds us; there is also an enchantment within us.

Humanity has been granted another gift; another power, if you will. It is a power that no other creature in the world possesses, a power that we cannot fully comprehend and often wield in foolish or trivial ways.

I am referring to the power of our words.

In the creation poem recorded in Genesis, God begins his creation act with a simple command: "Let there be light." (Genesis 1:3 NLT)

Do you notice that God did not simply *think* the world into being? He did not wave a magic wand, He did not sculpt it from some material, He did not paint it upon a canvas.

In the opening scene of our story, we find God **speaking words**, and light appears. Within the spoken word of God was the power and energy to create the universe.

If our Creator creates with words, they are something to pay attention to.

Humans are the only creatures who can speak. This is not merely a matter of intelligence, and it is not simply for the benefit of our communication.

Words CREATE. And words can destroy.

Our words hold an enchanted power that we must wield well.

The book of wisdom, Proverbs, tells us this:

> *The tongue can bring death or life;*
>
> *those who love to talk will reap the consequences.*
>
> Proverbs 18:21 NLT

We face a choice, then, as we set forth from the forest to pioneer in the field.

Will we use the power of our tongue to bring death or to create life?

If we choose to bring death with our words, it will sound like words of dishonor and ridicule. It can also sound like words of foolishness or lies. It can sound like judgement, criticism, cynicism, and other sorts of statements that bring discouragement and despair to those who hear them. If we are not aware of the power of our words, we can speak these things into existence without even intending to do so.

The most dangerous damage that can come from our own words is inflicted upon our own lives. The words we say or think about ourselves are often the most cruel and hopeless of all. Do not fall prey to the darkness when it comes to the power of your words, Young Traveler. There is magic within you! May you wield it well.

When you choose to bring life and light with your words, it will sound like words of possibility and hope. It will sound like words of empathy, compassion, forgiveness, and grace. It will sound like words of acceptance, for others and for yourself. Words of life are filled with wisdom and truth.

Hear me on this: the enchantment of our words does not mean that we must bolster up false positivity about things that we perceive as broken or breaking. But we can SPEAK THE HOPE of their restoration.

We can choose life.

We can choose blessing.

The power of our words will participate in the restoration.

That is the magic of hope.

It is contagious. It is transformative. It is LIGHT.

If you do not wish to take my word for it when it comes to the power of our words, you might care to note the wise ponderings of a certain Hogwarts Headmaster:

> *"Words are, in my not-so-humble opinion, our most inexhaustible source of magic. Capable of both inflicting injury, and remedying it."*[5]

I must add one final comment on the enchantment within you: words are only the beginning.

Like the boy in the story who received his full sight by the sacrifice of his father, we, too, have the opportunity for divine enchantment to live within us. We are invited to receive the Spirit of the Living God to dwell within our souls. The sacrifice of Jesus Christ made this possible, and presented us with the choice: will we receive the sacred mystery of Love itself, alive within us?

When we do, Young Traveler, the invisible realm becomes less hidden to our senses. We can sense the thin places, the places where the light is brighter or the darkness darker. We can navigate these woods about us and this field ahead of us with more wisdom, courage, and sight. May we be brave enough to receive this sight and to cultivate its flourishing.

The Stories You Will Tell

Of all the stories you will tell, it is my suspicion that the stories of enchantment will be the most beautiful parts of your tale.

Will you tell the stories of the thin places, where beauty is so real and palpable that it calls you to see the world beyond the world? Will you tell the stories of darkness defeated, where you wielded the power of the light? Will you tell the stories of the words of life that flow from your mouth and into the hearts of those you love, moving them towards hope and healing? Will you tell the stories of a God alive within you, restoring your sight and forming you to look like Love?

Always remember: YOU ARE ENCHANTED. YOU ARE POWERFUL. YOU ARE A PIONEER.

I'll Find You

I am made for wilderness
For the long treks in silence
For the strange gift of loneliness
For the thrill of awareness at the sounds

In the trees above
And the waters below
And the forest beyond

I found You in the wilderness
Because You are wild
And I am wild, too
In the wilderness, You call me

Brave
Beloved
Beautiful

I am made for mountains
For the crisp air of the morning
For the steep climbs to the summits
For the breathtaking wonder

Of the peaks above
And the valleys below
And the ranges beyond

I found You on the mountain
Because You are strong
And I am strong, too
In the mountains, You call me

Present
Powerful

Poet

I am made for home
For the steady, ordinary rhythms
For the work and the rest
For the unspeakable joy

Of authentic community
And faithful friendships
And cherished family

I'll find You at home
Because You are love
And I am love, too
At home, You call me

Helper
Healer
Holy

Until one day
When the mountains and wilderness become my home
Either in this world or the next
I'll find You
In whatever place I find myself

Chapter Three

A Story of Connection

I will hold your hand, love
As long as I can, love
Though the powers rise against us.
Though your fears assail you
And your body may fail you
There's a fire that burns within us.
And we dream in the night
Of a city descending
With the sun in the center
And a peace unending
I will carry the fire for you

Andrew Peterson

Once upon a time there lived a baker. He was a common sort of baker, the sort who woke early in the morning and worked hard in his kitchen so that when the townspeople came to market, he would have plenty of fresh bread to sell. He enjoyed his work, especially the happy faces of his customers when they bit into a loaf of his warm, hearty bread. The baker grew tired each evening after the long days of baking and selling, but he carried on in his profession, day in and day out, as all common bakers do.

One day, he was surprised to see a royal carriage pulling up to his shop. What could the palace guard be doing here? Had they come to buy his bread?

A tall, kind-looking gentleman robed in purple approached his door. This was not the king, no, but he did have the look of someone important. His graying hair and wrinkled eyes gave the baker assurance that whatever this man's job was, he had been doing it for quite some time.

The baker opened his door wide and bowed low to greet the tall man.

"Good morning, and welcome!" he greeted from his bowed position. "How may I help the royal court today?"

"Such honor you show me," said the man, smiling. "I am Sir Peter, the royal steward. The king has sent me to ask for your help on this fine day."

"The KING?" startled the baker, reeling back in surprise. "The king has asked for *my* help? Well, of course! Of course, Sir Peter, whatever can I do to be of service?"

"The king would like you to bake ten of your very finest loaves of bread for a feast he plans to hold tomorrow evening. He requests the honor of your company at the feast, and that you simply bring the bread with you."

"Me!" exclaimed the baker. "The king wants to eat MY bread for his feast?! Yes, yes of course, I will bake the finest bread anyone has ever tasted! I will bake bread fit for a king!"

The steward smiled warmly. "Just your usual bread will do well," he said. "Thank you for your service to the king."

With that, Sir Peter turned and walked regally back towards the carriage.

The baker slowly closed the door and took a couple deep breaths before letting out a yelp of glee. What a grand invitation! What an important honor! The king had called upon *him* for a favor, and this was the most meaningful, powerful, essential day of his life! The king would be eating *his* bread and serving it to the royal court!

The baker quickly closed his shop for the day, determining that nothing would distract him from baking the finest bread for the king. Everything was put on hold so that all his efforts could go into this most auspicious quest. As the baker began to prepare his ingredients and clean his kitchen to get ready for the baking that would begin at dawn, he imagined all sorts of honors and adulations that would begin to come his way. Why, the whole town would be jealous. Bakers across the land would come to learn from his mastery! People would be lining up for his autograph! The king would bring him into the palace to become the royal baker!!!

With that, the baker began to think about what he would pack to move into the palace. He imagined closing down his shop. He imagined having servants at the palace that would clean for him and prepare his meals. Oh, the great and glorious things that were on the horizon!

The next morning, the baker remained sequestered in his shop, all his energy and attention upon these ten loaves of bread that would be fit for the king. He decided to bake one hundred loaves, and then bring the finest ten. And so, he did, and he was incredibly pleased with the results.

"Beautiful!" he exclaimed as he gently placed the loaves of bread into his cart. "And now, we are off to the castle!"

The baker opened his door and wheeled his cart out into the street. To his surprise, he saw his neighbor, the butcher, wheeling a cart topped with a large, roasted boar in the same direction.

"Good morning!" the butcher called out to him. "I see you are off to the castle, too!"

The baker furrowed his brow for a moment. Had the king invited the butcher to bring meat for the feast? His merriment lessened in the realization that he was not the only one from his town that had been called upon for a favor by the king. Then again, the butcher always had quality meat. And of course, a feast would require meat! Nevertheless, bread was most assuredly more important than meat. It was still a special day, after all.

"Yes, well, out of my way, if you please," he said awkwardly. "I have an important delivery for the king." He continued towards the castle without a backwards glance, still dreaming of the moment when the king would honor him before the whole town.

But as he looked upon the road before him, he began to see others on their way to the castle. Why, there was a farmer, with a cart full of vegetables. And there was the chef from down the street, with a pot full of steaming soup. He looked behind him and saw his neighbor, a simple housewife, with an apple pie.

He began to understand that this was not the sort of feast he had first imagined. And this was not the sort of honor he had first imagined. Was the whole town summoned to prepare something for the feast?

The baker began to feel a scowl taking over his features. He tried to comfort himself, tried to assure himself that he was still special. He was bringing the bread, after all.

Just then, he saw something that made his heart sink. There at the entrance to the castle was an immense line of travelers, carting all sorts of offerings. This was not just his town... why, this was a feast for the whole country! As he looked, he saw a cart full of bread. And then another. And then another. It seemed that many other bakers had also been invited to bring bread to the feast.

His bread wasn't special. He wasn't special. And he could likely forget moving into the palace, after all.

Just then, he saw Sir Peter walking down the line, welcoming the travelers to the feast and thanking them for their offerings.

"You fooled me!" he called out to the steward. "You told me that my bread was a special favor for the king!"

Sir Peter looked at the baker's angry face and approached him kindly. "Ah, but this *is* a gift to the king! You see, the king wanted to host a feast for the whole country. Of course, in order to have enough food to feed the whole country, the king needed everyone who had something to give to bring it to the table. And so you have, dear baker. The king will be most grateful for your contribution."

"But I thought this bread was for the king!" the baker whined. "I worked all day to bake the very finest! I did not know it would just be a free feast for my neighbors!"

"*Imagine* the feast that awaits us," the steward said with a kind but reproachful tone, holding up his hand in a gesture of pause. "Imagine the bounty that shall be on those great tables ahead. Every person in the country, preparing the best they have to offer. Every garden, every grove, every forest, every hearth, coming together as one to create the most delicious, most diverse, most delightful feast that has ever been or ever will be!"

The baker paused for a moment, considering the words of the steward. Surely, he was right. If everyone had prepared food fit for a king, then they were certainly in for the greatest feast in the land.

"And you, fine baker," the steward continued, "you will have participated in the creation of this feast. Because you are here, it is better. It is more complete."

The baker nodded again. This was the finest bread he had ever baked. Certainly, the feast was better because he had chosen to come.

"And as for your neighbors," the steward continued, "who would you rather share such an experience with? The people who love you, who live with you, who care for you... would such a feast not be made better by sharing it with your neighbor?"

The baker's eyes welled up with tears. Of course, the wise steward had spoken truly. They were about to partake in the most glorious experience of life. One where everyone should be invited.

He reached out to take the steward's hand in gratitude. "Thank you," he said humbly. "I almost let this feast become about me.

Now I can see the truth... the feast has always been about everyone."

The False Story

Young Traveler, I wonder if this story rings true in your heart and experience? I imagine it does, for this story illuminates another falsehood that has wrought its ruin among the people of our modern age.

The false story is this: **You are alone and at the center of your story.**[6]

Like the baker, we humans tend to buy into this idea that we are at the center of our stories. That ours is the role of the hero, the protagonist, the one around whom all the plotlines and story arcs revolve. We tend to believe that the greatest experience we can have in life is the grand climax of our own narrative.

This false story has corrupted us into terribly selfish creatures. We have lost empathy for the stories of others, especially when they do not serve to further our own. We see the world from our own point of view, and lean away from projects or plotlines that clash with our own perspectives.

The problem with being at the center of our own stories, aside from the fact that it makes us selfish creatures, is that we find ourselves alone. The baker in our story shuts out the world to reach the pinnacle of his narrative. He almost lost the capacity to care about others, to celebrate their invitation to the feast, to feel grateful about their contributions. Where were his friends and family in the story? We do not know, because his story had become only about him.

What a lonely life that would be, to be alone and at the center of our stories.

And yet, that is a false story. Let me tell you what is true.

The True Story

The True Story is so much bigger than our individual experiences and lonely existence at the center of a false narrative. The True Story is that **we are created to flourish in an interconnected community**. The True Story is that the feast is not just for us. The feast is for everyone!

What is at the center of our stories, then? If they do not revolve around us, then who?

The center of the one True Story is the God who created us. The weight of the world rests upon His shoulders, not ours. The end of the story will be His doing, not ours. The feast of redemption will be at His table, not ours. And this allows us to rest in the knowledge that all shall be well.

From that knowledge, from that center point of existence, we can then begin to look at life as an opportunity for interconnection. Like the baker in the story, we can bring our best to the feast. While there are many other parts to the feast besides our personal loaves of bread, our bread is still important, valuable, welcomed, wanted. We can celebrate the beauty of our own becoming while also cheering on others who are bringing their best to the table.

This forest is too treacherous, and the field ahead too incalculable, for you to make the passage alone. Pioneers must travel together, for each brings their own strengths and weaknesses to the journey. Each brings their own food to the feast.

The Fellowship of the Ring

J.R.R. Tolkien helps us remember the one True Story in his trilogy, *The Lord of The Rings*. While there is a central character that serves to move the plotline forward – a dear little hobbit named Frodo – there are hundreds of other characters who play essential roles in the telling of the tale.

In the first book, *The Fellowship of the Ring*, Frodo himself begins with some influences of the false story. You see, Frodo volunteers for the most difficult and dangerous of all quests: to destroy the ring of power in the fires of Mount Doom. The hobbit demonstrates great courage in his willingness to accept this perilous mission, but he assumes that this journey is one that he must make alone. By making this assumption, he puts himself alone and in the center of his story.

And yet, a contingent of pioneers choose to bravely accompany Frodo on his journey: his best friend, Sam; two other hobbits, Merry and Pippin; the dwarf, Gimli; the men, Aragorn and Boromir, the elf, Legolas; and the wizard, Gandalf. Such a collection of races had never assembled before this grand undertaking, and Frodo finds it difficult to trust that they will see it through.

His friend, Sam, consoles him and tells him they are determined to join him on the quest:

> *"You can trust us to stick to you through thick and thin – to the bitter end. And you can trust us to keep any secret of yours – closer than you yourself keep it. But you cannot trust us to let you face trouble alone, and go off without a word. We are your friends, Frodo. Anyway: there it is. We know most of what Gandalf has told you. We know a good deal about the Ring. We are horribly afraid–but we are coming with you; or following you like hounds.'* [7]

And so, the Fellowship of the Ring was formed, and with it, a story much richer than any story about a single hobbit. As the tale continues, the fellowship is broken apart and scattered into groups, all fighting in their own ways for the destruction of the ring and the salvation of their people from the evil that seeks to enslave Middle Earth.

Frodo continues to struggle with the weight of the burden he carries, and he continues to struggle with the idea that he must do it alone.

In the end, it becomes most clear to Frodo that without the interconnected stories of the fellowship, without the love and sacrifice and courage and conviction of not only his friends but also thousands of elves, dwarves, and men, he could not be successful in his mission.

If the ring is to be destroyed, *it will take all of them*. That is the True Story.

The Skills of Interconnection

Yes, Young Traveler, there is a particular set of skills that will aid you as you seek to live a life of interconnection. Let us consider them for a few moments together as we sit by the fire.

The first skill is listening.

We could study this skill for many nights around the fire, for there is much to learn about listening. Since our time together is short, I will share with you just the beginnings of what you must know.

Perhaps you have heard of the story of the Madrigal family, an enchanted family from Columbia.[8] It is about a family who is – among other things – learning to listen to each other. Through their struggles, adventures, and victories, they learn about living as an interconnected family.

The Abuela in this story has a great amount of wisdom. She is trying to protect her family, save her family, instruct her family, and help them to flourish and by doing so provide and care for the whole village around them. She is also, in fact, trying to protect their miracle. When they listen to her advice and instruction, they gain wisdom.

Another character, Bruno, has a unique perspective. Sometimes it is important to listen to others, not necessarily for instruction, but because they see something *differently* than you do. That is called perspective. Perspective is essential for us to grow and to have healthy relationships with the people around us. Bruno does not see things from the same perspective as everyone else, but once the others hear his perspective, it begins to bring healing to the whole family.

A third character, Mirabel, listens out of love. She loves her family deeply, and she is on a mission to reunite them. She chooses to hear all their narratives and to love each person who shares their part of the story. The love she shows her family begins to rekindle the miracle, and they reunite as an interconnected and enchanted family. You see, the miracle is not about any one member of the Family Madrigal. *The miracle is all of them.*

Here are some simple truths about the essential skill of listening:

To listen is to love. To listen is to show another person that their presence, their words, and their experience matter. To listen is to gain insight and perspective, and to discover that others have things to teach you. When you listen, you choose to build a bridge between yourself and another person. That bridge can help you be prepared to communicate well, and that bridge can be a space of love and acceptance.

Listening requires curiosity. When you choose to listen to another person, you are choosing to remain curious about their perspective and experience. As they share that with you, do not forget to ask questions about what they are saying. Dig deeper, and work to understand their heart. When you do, you will discover the deep joy and fulfillment of an interconnected life. Curiosity will build more bridges than conviction ever will.

There is one last essential note on listening, Young Traveler. **Listening requires silence.** One cannot hear what another person is saying if one does not cease trying to be heard.

The wise Stephen Covey said it this way:

"Seek first to understand, then to be understood."[9]

Find a still place, Young Traveler, and learn to listen.

The second skill is empathy.

This is an experience that goes beyond listening, because sometimes a person cannot speak the feelings they are experiencing. Sometimes, a person needs someone to imagine what life must be like in their shoes. Sometimes, a person needs to believe that their feelings and experiences are valid, real, and worthy of someone's care.

Pioneers thrive when they can learn empathy.

In the powerful story, To Kill a Mockingbird, Harper Lee says it like this:

> *"If you can learn a simple trick, Scout, you'll get along a lot better with all kinds of folks. You never really understand a person until you consider things from his point of view, until you climb inside of his skin and walk around in it."* [10]

The field ahead will require empathy, and the world will thank you for it.

The third skill is collaboration.

To collaborate simply means to work together. This may sound easy enough, but this is becoming a lost art form in our modern world. When everyone believes that they are alone and at the center of their stories, they have a tough time allowing others to join them in the center.

When we can remember that we are not alone, and that we are not at the center, we position ourselves for a beautiful experience of collaboration. We are ready to enjoy all the food that is brought to the feast.

Instead of giving you advice about how to collaborate well, I am going to tell you how to destroy collaboration: comparison and competition. Comparison is that insidious feeling that urges you to measure your work, looks, friends, ideas, home, family, job, grades, and anything else you can fathom against someone else's. Comparison draws a "greater than" or "lesser than" sign between you and someone else. This is foolishness, and it will destroy collaboration. Competition is what follows from comparison; it is the insatiable drive to be the best, to have the best, and to draw the greater than sign always emanating from yourself, at the center.

If you can avoid these two practices, and if you can learn to listen and to empathize, you will lead a generation of people through the field ahead of you.

The great pioneer of the early church, Paul, puts it like this:

Galatians 6:4-6 MSG

> *Make a careful exploration of who you are and the work you have been given, and then sink yourself into that. Don't be impressed with yourself. Don't compare yourself with others. Each of you must take responsibility for doing the creative best you can with your own life. Be very sure now, you who have been trained to a self-sufficient maturity, that you enter into a generous common life with those who have trained you, sharing all the good things that you have and experience.*

May you share all the good things with your fellow pioneers, Young Traveler, in a generous common life of adventure in the field ahead.

The Stories You Will Tell

The ancient scripture uses the metaphor of a home or a temple to describe the interconnection that we are meant to participate in.

Ephesians 2:19-22 MSG

> *That's plain enough, isn't it? You're no longer wandering exiles. This kingdom of faith is now your home country. You're no longer strangers or outsiders. You belong here, with as much right to the name Christian as anyone. God is building a home. He's using us all—irrespective of how we got here—in what he is*

building. He used the apostles and prophets for the foundation. Now he's using you, fitting you in brick by brick, stone by stone, with Christ Jesus as the cornerstone that holds all the parts together. We see it taking shape day after day—a holy temple built by God, all of us built into it, a temple in which God is quite at home.

What stories will you tell, Young Traveler, as you pioneer the path ahead?

Will you tell the stories of a band of adventurers, working together to accomplish a common mission? Will you tell the stories of families reunited, of empathy offered and miracles witnessed? Will you tell the stories of how loved you felt when someone listened well, or of how you loved others by offering your ear to them?

Above all, I pray you will tell the stories of the feast, where everyone is invited, and where everyone is welcome, and where everyone leaves full.

Always remember: YOU ARE CONNECTED. YOU ARE NOT ALONE. YOU ARE A PIONEER.

Arms Locked

Arms locked
Hands clasped
Positioned for a wrestling match
Readied for a forceful clash

Shoulder opposite shoulder
My strength pitted against your strength
My story trumping your story

Muscles twitching
Body tensing
Poised for conflict
With each other

Arms locked
Hands clasped
Standing in a lined defense
Readied for a fierce attack

Shoulder to shoulder
My strength added to your strength
My story supporting your story

Muscles steady
Body ready
Poised for victory
We stand together

Chapter Four

A Story of Stewardship

Every place had been displaced, every love
unloved, every vow unsworn, every word unmeant
to make way for the passage of the crowd
of the individuated, the autonomous, the self-actuated, the homeless
with their many eyes opened toward the objective
which they did not yet perceive in the far distance,
having never known where they were going,
having never known where they came from.

Wendell Berry

One day, a young man traveled across the country to his mother's home. His father had recently died, and he was determined to help his mother take care of the house she had cherished for many long years. He arrived to see the home in pristine condition. The paint on the outside was fresh, and the lawn well-manicured. The garden was in full bloom, displaying a variety of flowers, vegetables, and berries. The fence, the storage shed, and the grounds had been tended with the utmost care.

As his mother welcomed him inside, he could see that the

interior matched the exterior. Her kitchen was spotless, her living room inviting, her dining room looked ready to hold a feast. Fresh flowers decorated the tables, and the scent of lavender filled his senses. He breathed deeply and felt a surge of joy. Everything here was as it had always been since he could first remember it.

He was home. He was grateful. He was at peace.

"You've kept the place looking beautiful!" he said kindly to his mother. "It must be so much work!"

She looked at him patiently and smiled. "Keeping our home lovely is my favorite work to do. When peace and beauty flourish around us, peace and beauty thrive within us."

They lived there together for some time, and the longer the young man stayed, the more peaceful and grateful he felt. Then, one day, his mother got an urgent message that her sister was ill.

"I must go and care for her," his mother said. "Will you stay here and take care of our home while I am away?"

"Of course, I will, mother," he agreed. "Take as much time as you need. I will see to the upkeep of everything here."

And so, she left, and the young man took on the responsibility to steward the property. But it turned out that it was a lot more work than he had bargained for. He tried to keep up with things, but with his mother gone, he had time for other pursuits. He took a job in town, telling himself that he would earn the money to hire some help for the house. When he returned home in the evenings, he was too tired to do much cleaning or caring for the home. The peace that had once filled him began to ebb away, replaced by a nagging stress. He felt an urgency to earn more money so that he could hire someone to help get the place back in order.

Slowly, the garden began to die off. He just could not remember to water it, and they had so little rain. His hours were picking up at work, and he certainly had no time for gardening! He tried to harvest what he could, telling himself that he would help his mother replant it in the fall.

One day, his friends came by for a visit. They traipsed through the door without removing their shoes, bringing dirt and debris through the hall and into the living room. They spread pizza boxes around the room and spilled sauce on the sofa. Before he could stop them, they pulled out beer and cigars, banishing the lingering lavender scent with the strong smells of their indulgences. The young man knew he should ask them to respect his mother's home, but it all felt out of his control.

The following week, a neighbor stopped by with a truck full of miscellaneous items.

"This stuff belonged to the garden club, and your dad was the president. The club is shutting down now since he is no longer with us, and we supposed it was your responsibility to tend to the mess he left behind."

The young man tried to protest, but before he could stop it, a whole truckload of junk had been unloaded in the front yard. He knew he should sort through it, but he was so exhausted from work. He needed to distract himself from this chaos, so he left the mess in the yard and went to watch TV.

Before long, a storm came through. The neighbors warned the young man to prepare for the storm, but he was too busy and too stressed and far too overwhelmed to do so. The wind was wild, and it broke the glass in his mother's kitchen window, shattering it across the floor. It spread the junk in the front yard around the property, covering the now-tall grass with assorted trinkets and trash.

The young man was heartbroken. How had this beautiful home become such a mess? It was just so out of his control. He was so busy, all the time. He was so tired, all the time. And he just had no way to regulate who and what showed up to make their messes. He felt angry, and exhausted, and so very overwhelmed.

The next morning, to his great dismay, his mother came home. She slowly walked through the trash-strewn patch of weeds and waste that was once her yard. She entered her home, taken aback by the smell and the mess all about. But she did not stop to comment on what had become of her home.

She rushed to her son, taking his weary face in her hands, and said, "My boy, what happened?"

A tear traced her cheek as the young man recounted the stories of all that had transpired. He fished around in his pockets, pulling out some stray cash that he offered to his mother to help get the place turned around again. His own eyes filled with tears of shame as he realized how deeply he had failed her request to care for their once-beautiful home.

"Now then," she said, pushing away the offered money and smiling kindly through her tears. "We can always restore the beauty of our home. That is merely the work of our hands. What is most important to me is restoring the peace in my son, for that is the work of the heart. Remember, when peace and beauty flourish around us, peace and beauty thrive within us."

They embraced, and as she held him close, he caught the faint scent of lavender once again.

The False Story

Young Traveler, you may sometimes feel like the man in this story. He longed for beauty, and had witnessed it, and yet when he was left to steward it, he let other things control the environment that he was trusted to tend. In doing so, he bought into the false story that you have surely heard before: **You have no control of your environment, and it has no effect upon you.**

The distractions that draw us away from the good, true, beautiful things of life are loud and entertaining, to be sure. The attraction of wealth and prestige can certainly make us feel like we have more important things to do than tend to our spaces and our planet. Before long, we have friends feeding us junk food and strangers dumping messes in our yards. And when the storms of life come, we are not prepared to handle the chaos they create.

But this, my friends, is a false story. Let me tell you what is true.

The True Story

The mother in our story had learned something essential about our life in this world: when peace and beauty flourish around us, peace and beauty thrive within us. But you see, it is not up to this world to create the peace and beauty to flourish around us. The stewardship of this magnificent creation - and the curation of its many beauties - is up to us.

Here is the True Story that you must remember as you pioneer the way forward: **You are a steward and curator of an environment that will cultivate either your flourishing or your diminishing.**

Let us reflect for a moment on those two words: steward and curate.

A deep understanding of these things will serve you well on your journey.

To steward something is to care for something that does not belong to you. The idea of stewardship means that while you hold the responsibility to preserve and protect something, you do not possess the thing you are stewarding. Rather, you are caring for it in such a way that when its owner returns, you can humbly say, "I left it better than I found it."

You see, this world does not belong to us, but rather to the One who created it. From the very beginning of the one True Story, ours has been the task to steward this creation: to nurture, protect, and preserve it. I am not only referring to the land, the animals, and the plants of this world, though these things are essential to preserve and protect. I am referring to all that is good and true and beautiful. The people, the art, the stories, the poetry, the music, the buildings, the cultures that make up this place we call home.

Here is an important understanding: goodness, truth, and beauty cannot be possessed, but they can be stewarded. It is our joy as pioneers to take this task most seriously.

And that brings us to our second word: curate. To curate something is to carefully select it from a variety of sources, to engage in the process of searching, discovering, gathering, choosing, and celebrating something. As pioneers, we also must embrace this second part of the task.

Not everything in this world is good, true, or beautiful. There is a growing assortment of garbage, a messy accumulation of excess waste, excess indulgence, excess darkness. There is much in this world that will try to tell you a false story rather than the true one. Like the young man caring for his mother's home, we may be fooled into thinking that we have no control over what we allow into our environment. We may even fool ourselves into thinking that our environment does not have much influence upon us.

But we are not fools. We are pioneers.

Consider these words from the ancient scriptures, written by the Apostle Paul, who taught many pioneers how to live and think rightly:

Philippians 4:8-9 NLT

> *And now, dear brothers and sisters, one final thing. Fix your thoughts on what is true, and honorable, and right, and pure, and lovely, and admirable. Think about things that are excellent and worthy of praise. Keep putting into practice all you learned and received from me—everything you heard from me and saw me doing. Then the God of peace will be with you.*

Do you notice his promise?

Peace.

Ah yes, just like the young man in the story, we long for peace. It is our natural habitat. It is our home. It is what we shall fully experience at the end of the one True Story.

As you think about this work of stewardship and curation, it may feel daunting. But just like the mother in the story, the more you practice it, the easier and more enjoyable it becomes.

In this moment, it may feel too challenging to resist the onslaught of media and messaging that assaults us from every side. It may feel too embarrassing to say no to behaviors or friendships that do not add peace and beauty around us. It may feel too exhausting to carefully consider everything we watch, everything we read, everything we consume, everything we surround ourselves with.

But I urge you to practice your callings, as a steward and a curator. Think wisely and carefully about how you can leave each place and person better than you found them. Think cleverly and cautiously about what sort of content and excess you allow into your life, your heart, your mind. The more you practice, the more peace and strength you will find.

In the field ahead, you will require all the peace and strength and beauty and truth you can find to pioneer the way forward.

Poison Poppies and Truffula Trees

You may have heard the story of the *Wizard of Oz*. Dorothy and her friends are traveling on a mission to the Emerald City. After passing through the forest and crossing the river, they come to a field of poppies. It appears beautiful, so they frolic ahead into the field, not considering what sort of effect this environment may have on them. As they begin to walk along through the field, they start to feel drowsy. Finally, Dorothy, her dog, and her friend the Lion all fall asleep. Were it not for her friends and a fierce contingent of field mice who carried them out of the field, they may have slept there forever.

It is easy for the false stories to lull us to sleep, Young Traveler. And so, we must remain vigilant, aware of our surroundings and how they are influencing us.

The great Dr. Seuss once told a story of the Lorax, a creature who spoke for the trees. The Lorax lives in a land where people have ceased caring for the environment around them. The business tycoons and the manufacturing moguls have done their worst upon the forests of Truffula Trees, and there is all but nothing left of a once beautiful forest.

In the story, a young boy comes upon the "Once-ler," who turns out to be the one whose greed spawned the destruction of the land and its once-beautiful creatures. The Once-ler tells the story of the Lorax who tried to stop him from destroying the beautiful environment around him, and how slowly all the trees and all the creatures disappeared from it. At the end of his tale, the Once-ler is alone in devastation, destruction, and terrible pollution. Even the Lorax disappears, leaving behind only one message: the word "UNLESS" carved into a stone.

"But now," says the Once-ler, "now that you're here,

the word of the Lorax seems perfectly clear.

UNLESS someone like you cares a whole awful lot,

nothing is going to get better. It's not."[11]

The Once-ler entrusts the last remaining Truffula seed to the boy and encourages him to replant the forest, to steward and curate an environment where the trees and creatures can flourish once again.

While this tale of Dr. Seuss can certainly be quite literal as we look at our planet and the destruction and pollution we face today, it can also be an allegory. There are other places in our environments that will also become destroyed and polluted unless we tend to them.

May we tend to them well, Young Travelers.

The Stories You Will Tell

I wonder what stories you will tell, Young Traveler, as you make your way through this forest?

I will leave you with this final scripture to contemplate. Another letter of Paul to the pioneers of his age:

1 Corinthians 4:1-2 NIV

> *This, then, is how you ought to regard us: as servants of Christ and as those entrusted with the mysteries God has revealed. Now it is required that those who have been given a trust must prove faithful.*

I pray you will tell the stories of beauty uncovered, and of goodness restored. I pray you tell the stories of goodness stewarded, and trust proven faithful. I pray you will tell the stories of sorting out trash from treasure, or of transforming something broken into something whole.

Most of all, I pray you will tell the stories of peace and joy in your soul as you go about this important work of stewardship and curation.

Always remember: YOU ARE A STEWARD. YOU ARE A CURATOR. YOU ARE A PIONEER.

God of the Garden

God of the Garden
You gifted us with your
True Affection
Whole Perfection
The beauty of Eden
Was a just glimpse of Your
Own Reflection

God of the Garden
We broke your trust with our
Prideful Rejection
Foolish Subjection
We deified ourselves
Our sin has cursed us with
Utter Dejection

God of the Garden
You chose to free us
Divine Revelation
Complete Salvation
Your love made flesh
Your Garden made new in
Your Restoration

God of the Garden
We steward this space
Faithful Conservation
Careful Curation
Awaiting Recreation
Guard and guide us
Form and inspire us
Your incarnation

Chapter Five

A Story of Wholeness

May you realize that the shape of your soul is unique,
that you have a special destiny here,
that behind the facade of your life
there is something beautiful, good, and eternal happening.
May you learn to see yourself with the same
delight, pride, and expectation
with which God sees you in every moment.

John O'Donohue

Once upon a time there lived a horse. He was the strongest, tallest, handsomest horse in all the land. Every day he would run through the meadow for hours, strengthening and stretching his muscles from dawn until dusk. He ate only the finest grasses and would never nibble on a sweet treat in the forest. He drank from the purest streams and found the most restful, silent places to sleep at night.

But the horse was foolish. He had no time for learning or stuady, and no sources of wisdom to help him increase his own.

And the horse was lonely. He had no friends who could keep up with his running, and he spent most of his days alone.

And the horse was sad. While he was the finest, fittest creature in the land, he had no purpose outside of his strong body.

One day, an owl perched upon a tree and spoke to the horse.

"You are a foolish creature," the owl taunted. "You spend all your time building up your muscles and strengthening your body, but what good will that do you when trouble comes? You should forget your body and strengthen your mind, like me."

The owl was the smartest creature in the forest, for the owl had dedicated his days to studying philosophy and learning about culture, history, math, and science. He could quote the greatest thinkers of all time, and he would spend hours reading each day. He carefully curated his learning and refused to allow foolish ideas to enter his mental space. He learned daily and wrote long journals of all the wisdom he had collected.

But the owl was weak. He did not care for his body, and he could fly only a short distance before becoming exhausted.

And the owl was lonely. In his effort to protect his mind from folly, he had driven his friends and family away.

And the owl was sad. His intelligence and study had not

brought him any great purpose for his life.

As the owl loomed in pride over the horse, a dog approached them.

"You've both got it wrong!" The dog laughed. "Look at you, lonely and friendless. All your work to strengthen your body and sharpen your mind has left you all alone! You should forget all that work and spend your time making friends!"

The dog was the most social creature in the forest, for the dog had dedicated his life to collecting friends. He would spend his days meeting new animals and inviting them to his home. He would share his food and stories with them, laughing and chatting until late in the evenings. He never met a stranger, and all the animals enjoyed his kindness and generosity.

But the dog was sick. All the food he ate with his friends was making him too heavy, and he couldn't get around the way he used to.

And the dog was silly. He liked to laugh with his friends, but he had never learned anything about the world and never stretched his mind.

And the dog was secretly sad. All the friends he collected never seemed like quite enough to fill the space inside of him.

As the dog continued to smirk at the horse and the owl, a tiger approached the group.

"You're all missing the mark," he taunted. "You think that your body or your mind or your friends will give you a happy life? All of it fades away. The only thing that really matters is being at one with the universe."

The tiger was the most spiritual creature in the forest, for the tiger had dedicated his life to pursuing mindfulness and meditation. He would spend his days walking alone in silence, contemplating spirituality and the meaning of life. He had no time for others, for he found peace and tranquility in his own pursuits of the divine.

But the tiger was frail, for he had never run like tigers are born to do.

And the tiger was foolish, for he had no time for learning from others.

And the tiger was lonely, for none of the other creatures wanted to be near him.

The animals looked at each other, wondering which of them was truly the most satisfied and fulfilled in life.

Just then, a lamb appeared from behind a tree.

"I think you're all lovely," the lamb said kindly. "You work hard at what is important to you, and you have each become great in your own ways. I wonder, though... what you could learn from each other?"

The animals gazed at the lamb. He was humble, and kind, and beautiful in his own way.

For the lamb was the happiest creature in the forest.

His body was strong, for he loved to run and play in the meadow every morning.

His mind was smart, for he took a few hours each evening to read and learn.

His friends were plentiful, for he always took care to be kind and respectful to everyone.

And his purpose was clear, for he never forgot that he was a creature, made by the Creator who loved him so.

The lamb was not the strongest, or the smartest, or the most popular, or the most spiritual.

The lamb was simply the most whole.

The False Story:

Dear pioneer, hear this well. You have been sold another false story of our modern age. The false story is this: **If you work**

hard enough at something, you will achieve success, happiness, and fulfillment.

Have you heard this story before? Yes, indeed, and so have we all. There is something particularly insidious about this false story, for it is remarkably close to the truth. The most damaging falsehoods are the ones that alter only a small portion of what is real.

And so, you may ask, isn't it wise to work hard? Aren't we created for accomplishment? Isn't it true that we can become all that we are created to be? Isn't it true that there is a vast array of potential that waits dormant inside every person, anticipating the day when we apply ourselves with dedication and determination to see it through?

Yes. All of that is true. It is the second part of the story that sends us off course.

This idea of success *does* have a place in our True Story, and in our becoming. But we find ourselves in grave danger of disaster if we begin to believe that success is the greatest aim of our lives. The horse, the owl, the dog, and the tiger in our story all achieved the highest degree of success in the areas of their strengths. And yet, the horse, the owl, the dog, and the tiger were not happy.

You have been told that if you work hard enough at something, you will be a success, and that by achieving success you will experience happiness and fulfillment.

While this may be a true statement, it is not a True Story. It is not a foundation to build your life upon. Let me tell you what is true.

The True Story

Hard work is essential in life, and succeeding in your endeavors is a wonderful experience on your way to becoming. And yet, here is the True Story you must always remember as you enter the field ahead: **Your aim is not success, but wholeness.**

The lamb in our story experienced success in every area of his life. He was healthy, he was wise, he had friends, and he had purpose. But the lamb's focus in life was not on his success in these areas. The lamb was becoming a whole creature, with attention given not just to a fragment of his being, but to all his being.

As a human creature, you inherently have separate areas of need. Biological, psychological, social, and spiritual. To attempt to live a flourishing life without attending to these areas will lead you toward exhaustion and frustration, not wholeness.

The time has come for me to tell you the *end of the story*. The one True Story, the story from which all these stories we share around the fire are derived.

The end of the one True Story is WHOLENESS.

The end of the one True Story is a creation restored to the fullness, beauty, and peace from which it came. It is a creation where there is no death, no sickness, no violence, no starvation, no evil, no suffering, no pain. It is a creation where God unites heaven and earth in a final act of redemption.

Here is how the apostle John wrote it in the book of Revelation:

Revelation 21:1 – 5 NIV

> *Then I saw "a new heaven and a new earth," for the first heaven and the first earth had passed away, and there was no longer any sea. I saw the Holy City, the new Jerusalem, coming down out of heaven from God, prepared as a bride beautifully dressed for her husband. And I heard a loud voice from the throne saying, "Look! God's dwelling place is now among the people, and he will dwell with them. They will be his people, and God himself will be with them and be their God. 'He will wipe every tear from their eyes. There will be no more death or mourning or crying or pain, for the old order of things has passed away."*
>
> *He who was seated on the throne said, "I am making everything new!" Then he said, "Write this down, for these words are trustworthy and true."*

May we never forget the end of the True Story as we journey through the middle.

This forest that surrounds us is not located at the end of the story. The field ahead is too vast for us to see whether or not it will contain the end of the story. Perhaps there will be yet another landscape beyond the field. But what we can be sure of is this: as we move forward in the one True Story, we move forward in a journey towards wholeness.

The way we move towards wholeness is to participate in it. Where something breaks, we mend it. Where something is weak, we strengthen it. Where something is hurting, we heal it. Where something is despairing, we bring hope. That is the aim of our journey as pioneers in the field ahead, and that is the aim of the God who created us. We join him in the work of wholeness.

A Wholeness Within Us

Having this glimpse of the end of the story then, how are we to live in this moment? Shall we give up on the pursuit of achievement and simply wait for all to be made new? Certainly not! Ours is the task to join in the movement towards wholeness, and that begins with a wholeness in ourselves.

Like the creatures in the story, we possess the capacity for strength, wisdom, and beauty. We are made to grow towards our whole selves and to accomplish important, significant things in this world! We are made for healthy flourishing in our physical, social, mental, and spiritual selves. How best shall we mark our movements towards wholeness in each of these essential areas of our lives?

We can begin to mark our movements towards wholeness in three ways: ***affirmation, achievement, and habit.***

Affirmation is a practice of speaking truth about your whole self. Affirmation allows you to envision the best version of your unique self, and to participate daily in the becoming of the person you are created to be. As you begin to speak life and meaning and intention into the person you are becoming, you will indeed become increasingly like the whole version of yourself.

I urge you to consider writing down some truths about your strengths. Take some time to consider others whom you may admire and want to emulate. Most importantly, look to Jesus, and consider the way he lived. As you consider what wholeness looks like for you, you will find ways of expressing it that you can carry with you into each day of your life.

Achievement is a wonderful way to celebrate milestones on your journey towards wholeness. Academics, physicality, employment, creative pursuits, and hobbies are all places where you can set specific and measurable goals. As you set these goals, consider carefully where the achievement of these goals will take you. Will it bring you closer to the expression of your whole self, of the person you are created to be?

If so, embrace these goals with energy and passion! Fill your mind and heart with visible, tangible reminders of the achievements you are pursuing. Work hard, committing yourself to the discipline and effort it will take to see them through. And celebrate those accomplishments with great rejoicing and reward! Marking your movements towards wholeness is an essential part of the journey.

Habit is the most indispensable piece of our movement toward wholeness. Our habits shape us in profound and indelible ways. As we choose to form and develop the habits of our lives, we are choosing to form and develop the people we become.

The most foolish way to form habits is to take no conscious action about them at all. If we do not purposefully and intentionally choose our habits, our lesser selves will form them. The parts of us prone to comfort, convenience, and complacency will not lead us towards wholeness. We will never grow into the full expression of the people we are created to be if we do not *choose* to do so.

What sort of habits mark the life of a pioneer on a journey toward wholeness?

Here is a concise list to help your imagination get started. Only you can choose the habits that are essential for you.

Physical habits:

- Daily exercise
- Daily hydration
- Healthy eating choices

Mental habits:

- Journaling
- Mindfulness breathing
- Time outside in nature

Social habits:

- One meal a day with others
- Limited technology use to create space for presence with people
- Weekly investment into a community

Spiritual habits:

- Daily scripture reading

- Daily prayer
- Weekly gathering with a church community

If you are as perceptive as I believe you are, you may be feeling that these three areas – affirmation, achievement, and habit – are not enough to bring us true wholeness. Your feeling is most certainly correct. We will need more to guide us on our journey of wholeness. Wait with me here at the fire a while longer, and I will tell you what I know.

A Wholeness Around Us

As you become a whole person, you will begin to long for wholeness around you. You will learn to recognize the spaces and people moving towards that wholeness, and you will learn to recognize the spaces and people moving *away* from that wholeness.

Pay attention to that awareness, Young Traveler. Choose wisely regarding the spaces and people with which you spend your time. Those spaces and people will form you, for better or for worse.

I pray that you, pioneer, shall be formed for the better.

Remember the end of the story, where everything is whole, and all is made new. Some scholars call this new creation the "Kingdom of God." The Kingdom of God already exists: it is the place of perfect beauty, perfect truth, perfect goodness. It is the place where God dwells, the place where we will one day find our rest and peace.

This quote from Frederick Buechner serves to remind us of what it looks like and feels like to glimpse that wholeness:

> *IF WE ONLY HAD eyes to see and ears to hear and wits to understand, we would know that the Kingdom of God in the sense of holiness, goodness, beauty is as close as breathing and is crying out to be born both within ourselves and within the world; we would know that the Kingdom of God is what we all of us hunger for above all other things even when we don't know its name or realize that it's what we're starving to death for. The Kingdom of God is where our best dreams come from and our truest prayers. We glimpse it at those moments when we find ourselves being better than we are and wiser than we know. We catch sight of it when at some moment of crisis a strength seems to come to us that is greater than our own strength. The Kingdom of God is where we belong. It is home, and whether we realize it or not, I think we are all of us homesick for it.* [12]

The Stories You Will Tell

I love to imagine the stories you will tell as you make your way through the field. I imagine they will be stories of art created, songs composed, and poetry written. I imagine they will be stories of races run, games won, and projects begun. I imagine they will be stories of grand adventures and great victories.

I imagine that you will teach a generation from the wisdom and experience you gain on your journey towards wholeness.

Always remember: YOU ARE BECOMING WHOLE. YOU ARE A PIONEER.

Broken Whole

I once thought growth
Happened in a straight line
Over time
Tenacity and grit
Expanding it
Into completion
And then I was beaten
Shattered and scattered
Across the acres of my years
My tears tell the story of
My ache
My break

Shall I put the pieces back together
Aligned and resigned
To becoming what used to be?
Old me?
Or shall there be something new that
Becomes of the broken
Something different awoken
Something the whole of me
Longed to be
Beyond the reaches of my capacity

What mosaic shall I make
Of these loves and longings?
These cares and callings?
What shall I form
From the torn places and battered spaces?
And if I dare to pair
These pieces anew
Will I be judged and mocked?
Will I be scorned and blocked?

Something waits at the gates
Of my guarded heart
A spark
A power that comes to restore
Even more
Than what has been lost
No matter the cost
A song
Rises and ripples through the
Fog of my pain
And again
I sing along

Oh God I break
So You can remake
My soul
A broken whole

Chapter Six

A Story of Virtue

A loving heart was better and stronger than wisdom.

Charles Dickens

Once upon a time in a faraway land there lived a chief who thought himself to be extremely wise and incredibly brave. The chief had stepped into power upon the passing of his father, and he held his role as the leader of his tribe with a great amount of pride. He was determined to lead his people with a firm hand, a stout heart, and a cunning mind.

The tribe made their home in a lush valley. They were known as hunters and farmers, flourishing for generations with plenty of food to eat and to trade. They lived a happy, simple, humble life, but this life was not enough for the new chief. He longed for his tribe to become the most powerful tribe in the land.

One day, he decreed that the tribe would be relocating to the base of a mountain to the east. From this location, with a great forest nearby as a resource, they could expand their farming capabilities as well as begin the production of weapons for conquest.

The chief's younger brother stood in opposition to this plan. "Brother, why would we uproot our people from a happy, simple life? What need do we have for power and conquest?"

"You are a fool!" The chief spat at his brother, looking down upon him with contempt. "You know nothing of ruling a tribe, nor of power! I will make our tribe great and mighty, and you will see how wise I am!"

The younger brother argued again. "What proof do you have that this new land will be any better than where we are now? What if a move leaves us less safe and less happy than we are here?"

The chief laughed mockingly. "Your fear will leave you powerless and useless, brother. Take a lesson from me. I am not afraid of the unknown, and I am confident we will be better off on the new land."

And so, against the wishes of the people, the chief moved the village to the base of the mountain. They replanted their crops and began to reap the forest in preparation for the fashioning of weapons.

The chief's brother was in charge of scouting, sent to survey the land and report back with information on resources and other tribes who may be vulnerable to attack. One day, their party ascended the mountain a short distance to get a perspective from higher ground. As they gazed across the land, one of the scouts looked up to the peak of the mountain and let out a terrified yelp.

"Smoke!" he cried urgently, pointing to the summit. The scouts looked up to see the faint but unmistakable tendrils of smoke rising from the top of the mountain.

The tribe had made their new home at the base of a volcano.

The chief's brother mounted his horse and galloped all the way back to the village as quickly as the animal could carry him.

"Brother!" he called, rushing into the chief's tent. "We must leave this land at once! We have settled at the base of a volcano!"

The chief looked up from his meal, which he was happily indulging in at midday, while his tribe was hard at work.

"Don't be preposterous!" the chief said smugly. "We have already scouted that mountain, and there are no signs of a volcano."

"The signs have come!" the brother retorted. "We saw smoke rising from the top of the mountain. We would be fools to ignore it."

"Fools?" thundered the chief, standing tall to overshadow his brother. "Do not dare to call me a fool, boy. I am no fool, and I am not afraid of a little smoke." The chief leaned in close. "Your gutless doubts will not get the best of my courage. We stay here, and I don't wish to hear another word about it."

With that, the chief dismissed his brother and went back to his meal.

The younger brother was heartbroken over the chief's decision, and angry at the foolish pride that could cost the lives of his friends and family in the village. The injustice of the folly was deeply troubling, and yet he did not wish to disrespect his brother or to start a rebellion in the tribe.

Instead, the younger brother decided to go seek counsel from his grandmother, the wisest and oldest member of their community.

After he had told her his story, she looked at him with a quiet strength and spoke with confidence. "Those who declare themselves to be the wisest and the bravest are sometimes the most blind to the truth. Your brother cannot see what is real, for he only sees what he desires to see."

"But what can I do?" the brother asked urgently. "We cannot stay here to be burned in the wake of an eruption. We cannot hide the truth of what our scouts saw. Am I to overthrow my own brother in order to save our people?"

The old woman smiled a patient, loving smile. "While your brother claims to be wise, you are the one who chooses to see what is real. That is the foundation of true wisdom."

"What good is my wisdom?" the young man burst out. "Our fool of a chief refuses to hear it, and he will lead us to our doom!"

"Peace, child," said his grandmother. "You must temper the anger you feel at the injustice of your brother's choices. You must instead choose courage, a courage that will right the wrongs your brother has caused. This courage shall not be born of anger, but of love. You love the people of your tribe, and because of that love you will fight for what is just."

The younger brother swallowed hard. His grandmother was asking a great deal of him. Asking for a greater degree of courage, love, wisdom, and faith than he currently possessed. And yet, as she spoke, he could feel something strengthening in him, something coming alive. He could not let his people die.

"There is it, young one," she said with a genuine expression of hope in her eyes. "I see the spark in you... the spark of a great leader and a virtuous man. Trust it, and go about the work you must do."

He clasped her hands and bowed his head in a gesture of gratitude, before swiftly moving out of the tent and back towards the village center.

"We have no time to waste," he spoke bravely to the scouting party who was waiting to hear their next instructions. "We must announce the truth to the village, and we must advise the people to pack their things. We are leaving today."

"The chief has decreed this?" one of the scouts asked, surprised.

"No," said the brother. "But it is what we must do."

"If you are going to undermine the chief, you must take his life," said the scout conspiratorially. "If you don't, he will surely take yours!"

"I will not take the life of my brother," the young man said decidedly. "What he chooses to do is his responsibility."

The scout's eyes grew wide, but there was something compelling about the resolve in the young brother of the chief. "Very well, then," said the scout. "We will spread the word."

The men moved quickly, warning the village in a calm urgency. People began packing and preparing to flee the site of what could certainly be a great tragedy.

It took several hours before the chief took notice of the flurry in the village. When he discovered the betrayal of his brother, he was furious. He called his guards together and instructed them to arrest the young man, his own brother, who had chosen this treachery.

The two faced off in the center of the village, the chief in a royal fury, the young brother in a poised calm, even with the spears at his back.

"You dare to defy me?" the chief fumed. "I will have your head for this!"

"Do you not realize, brother, that I could have taken your head? While you slept in your tent, weakened by your midday feasting and drinking, I could have taken your life and assumed your position as chief. But I do not want your title or your power. I do not want to hurt you or dishonor you. And yet, this village will burn if we do not relocate now. Look!" The young man pointed to the mountain, where the smoke was now billowing for all to see. "There is no time left, we must leave this place!"

The villagers gasped in horror, but the chief scoffed. "You are a traitor and a coward!" he shrieked. I will show you, I will show all of you how a brave and wise chief defends his village!" With that, the chief instructed his guards to follow him.

As they mounted their horses to ride towards the smoke, the chief called back, "We shall dig a trench so wide and deep that the molten rock will be directed around the village! Then you will see who is the wisest and the bravest among us!"

The young brother called out to stop him, but he would not turn back. The ground began to shake, and the brother turned his attention to moving the villagers to safety. It was only hours later that the mountain erupted, covering the valley with magma, fire, and smoke. The young brother had managed to save his village, but the chief and his men were never seen or heard from again.

The False Story

Another false story has crept into the narrative of our age, and it goes something like this: **humans should be free to do what is right in their own eyes.** You have surely come across this story, and perhaps you have told it. There is something compelling about a story of freedom. Indeed, humans *are* free and *should be* free.

And yet, humans left to do what is right in their own eyes, without having an accurate measure of *rightness*, have never succeeded in creating anything good or true or beautiful in the world. In fact, humans who overtly make up their own version of morality have been the humans to commit the greatest atrocities in our history. Holocausts, wars, starvation, conquest, abuse, and all kinds of evil have come from humans doing what is right in their own eyes.

The chief in our story fashioned his own sort of wisdom: a wisdom that was derived from his own desires and perspectives. While he could declare that he was brave and strong and wise and powerful, that did not make it true. While the chief was free to do what was right in his own eyes, that freedom led him to his doom.

Humans are indeed free. The insidious part of this story is the final part, the part which tells us that our own measures of wisdom and justice and rightness and goodness should be the measures by which we make our choices. This is a false story. Let me tell you what is true.

The True Story

What a gift it is to be free, to not be bound to a script we must follow or a part we must play. We have the boundless joy and honor of authoring our own stories, choosing our own paths, and making our own way. The true story is this: **humans are free to make choices; choices guided by virtue will lead us toward wholeness, and choices guided by vice will lead us toward destruction.**

The false story which tells us that we are free to do what is right in our own eyes forgets the reality that the good, true, and beautiful things of our world possess an inherent *rightness* and *wholeness* that is not determined by our choices, perspectives, or opinions. When God created the world, he defined what is good and true and beautiful. As humans, we don't define goodness, truth, or beauty. We reflect it. We seek it. We celebrate it in diverse ways, with opinions about it that are as vast as the stars in the sky.

In our story, the chief wanted to define his own rightness. He refused to see the truth that was right in front of him, and he refused to value the safety and happiness of his people. The chief chose what was right in his own eyes, and it led to his destruction. The brother, on the other hand, could see the truth of things. He had a sense of justice and goodness that was not based on his opinions or desires, but rather on a morality that existed beyond him. Because of the wise counsel of his grandmother, who had the clearest understanding of virtue, he had the courage and wisdom to save his village. His virtue led him toward wholeness.

Virtue is not something that we define or create. Virtue is something we can choose and embrace. When we choose the path of virtue, we choose the path of wholeness. When we choose the path of vice, like the chief in the story, we choose the path of destruction. Now, you may be wondering exactly what virtue and vice are. To answer that, we must travel back in time to the ancients.

Hercules at the Crossroads

Perhaps you have heard the stories of the ancient legend of Hercules. According to Greek and Roman tradition he was a hero, born a demigod, part mortal and part divine. Hercules went on many adventures and suffered many trials as he discovered his destiny and sought to take his place on Mount Olympus.[13]

There is a parable passed down through the centuries of a young Hercules, presented with a choice. Before he begins his adventures, Virtue and Vice, personified by beautiful women, meet him at a crossroad.

Vice, dressed in rich garments and jewels, offers him a life of pleasure: an easy, carefree, delightful life of indulgence and excess. Virtue, dressed in a simple white frock, offers him a life of hardship and honor. She tells him that while his journey with her will be glorious, it will be full of toil.

Hercules chooses the life of virtue, both the blessing and the pain.

It is certainly telling that even ancient teachers and philosophers understood virtue, and believed that an ultimate sense of goodness, truth, and beauty exists. The ancients may have told this parable to emphasize the value of glory and achievement, and to teach that it costs something to be honored. But there is a more important lesson embedded in this story.

The false story has been woven into the fabric of humanity since the dawn of civilization. Vice herself lies to Hercules from the very beginning. You see, vice is presented as a *choice that costs nothing*. The lie is that virtue is hard, but vice is easy. And the subtext is that humans should be free to choose either the "good and virtuous life" or the "easy and indulgent life".

Pioneer, do not be deceived here. *Everything costs something.* The cost of virtue is indeed toil, for there is hardship involved in self-discipline and courage and all the rest of the virtues. The younger brother of the chief found his path most difficult. But the cost of vice is more than mere hardship. The cost of vice is destruction. The chief thought he was living the good life, and he even thought himself to be wise and brave ... but in the end it meant his doom.

What then, does it mean to live a life of virtue? How shall we use our freedom to forge a path towards our wholeness?

The Four Cardinal Virtues

The ancient Greek philosophers distinguished four cardinal virtues. They are certainly an essential place to start as we consider a conversation about how to live well. The cardinal virtues are prudence, temperance, fortitude, and justice.

Prudence

The simplest way to explain prudence is this: ***to see what is real, and act accordingly.***

The medieval philosophers considered prudence, or as some may call it, wisdom, to be the "mother of all virtues". (Pieper reference) To understand the heart of prudence is to understand that the highest experience of human freedom is not to live "however we want". It is to choose to live well. To be prudent is to determine what is good, to identify a right action or choice. It is then to take that action and make that choice, for as Stephen Covey wisely put it:

> *"To know and not to do is not to know."* [14]

The chief's brother displayed a great degree of prudence in our story. Not only did he discover the truth about the volcano, but he discerned that to act accordingly would be to seek counsel, temper his anger at his brother, and evacuate the endangered area. Not only did he understand that these choices were wise, but he also took the steps necessary to enact them despite the personal cost.

This action required his embrace of the other virtues. Virtues tend to work together to help us in our movement toward wholeness.

Temperance

Temperance may also be referred to as self-control or self-discipline. Temperance can be explained in this way: ***to prioritize what IS good in the long term over what FEELS good in the short term.***

The chief had no degree of temperance. He moved his tribe to the base of a volcano without taking the necessary steps to ensure it was a safe place to live. He spewed anger and pride all over his brother with no regard to his feelings. He ate and drank in the middle of the day while his village was hard at work. And he impulsively charged toward an active volcano with the foolish notion that he could avert the coming doom. He could not see the long view, and his actions were based on what felt good in the moment.

The chief's brother displayed temperance by restraining the anger and frustration he felt at his brother and instead choosing to act rightly. He also displayed temperance by engaging in difficult conversations with his grandmother and his brother rather than ignoring the problem or impulsively reacting to it. This required a great degree of temperance, for human emotions are powerful things. However, a virtuous person can choose to see the long view, and to temper emotions or lesser needs for the greater good.

Justice

Justice is an ancient idea that has endured to make its way into our modern vocabulary. The explanation of justice is: ***to advocate for each person to have the honor, dignity, provision, consequence, and rights they deserve, in equal measure.***

We may think of justice when we think of our legal system, which exists to right wrongs, maintain equity, and punish those who would commit an injustice towards another person. We may also think of systemic justice, where a portion of a population is oppressed or abused, and we enter to restore what is fair and right.

The young brother in the story displays a sense of justice in many ways. He wants to give his community a safe place to live. He wants to honor his brother's leadership. He is willing to face consequences for his actions. Each of these movements towards justice is costly, but he chooses it out of an awareness that it is the right price to pay for the good of all.

Fortitude

Fortitude may also be referred to as courage or strength, but it is something more than that. Fortitude may be explained like this: ***to remain resilient and resolved to see the right thing through to the end.*** It takes courage and strength to advocate for the right thing, but it takes fortitude to see it through. Fortitude is courage and strength over time.

When we can see what is real and act accordingly, prioritize what is good in the long term over what feels good in the short term, and advocate for each person to have the honor, dignity, provision, consequence, and rights they deserve, in equal measure ... then we must also have fortitude, because these choices require courage and determination over time.

C.S. Lewis puts it best:

> *"Courage is not simply one of the virtues, but the form of every virtue at the testing point."* [15]

The young brother in the story had a great degree of fortitude. He did not flee for his own life when he saw the evidence of an imminent eruption. He did not back down when his brother mocked him and belittled him. He chose a path of resistance when he stood up to his brother. He saw the rescue of his village through to the end, despite the personal cost and threats to his life and comfort.

There is indeed much we can learn from the ancient and medieval thinkers who pioneered their own fields centuries before we were born. There is immense value in the cardinal virtues: prudence, temperance, justice, and fortitude. These virtues can help to guide you toward a life of wholeness, and it would serve you well to embrace them as you enter the field ahead.

And yet, we always turn to the source of greatest wisdom to anchor our learnings, so we will refer to another ancient text:

2 Peter 1:5-8 NLT

> *In view of all this, make every effort to respond to God's promises. Supplement your faith with a generous provision of moral excellence, and moral excellence with knowledge, and knowledge with self-control, and self-control with patient endurance, and patient endurance with godliness, and godliness with brotherly affection, and brotherly affection with love for everyone. The more you grow like this, the more productive and useful you will be in your knowledge of our Lord Jesus Christ*

As we can see, the apostle Peter also extolled the pursuit of virtue. But he implores us to remember that we do not exercise virtue for virtue's sake. There is something far more essential. **Virtue culminates in love.**

The Three Christian Virtues

There are many Christian virtues we could think about, and many you will need as you leave the forest for the field ahead. But to simplify our conversation, for I see our fire burning fast, we will advance to the most important three.

The apostle Paul says it simply and clearly:

1 Corinthians 13:13 NLT

> *Three things will last forever—faith, hope, and love—and the greatest of these is love.*

The three Christian virtues, considered by centuries of theologians to be the highest and most important of the virtues, are faith, hope, and love.

Faith

The ancient scriptures define faith as "confidence in what we hope for and assurance about what we do not see." (Hebrews 11:1 NIV). If we are to define it in this moment as you prepare to head into the field, we can define it as such: **to trust that God is good and that He loves us.**

A mistrust of this truth has been brooding and breeding throughout the ages of human existence. And surely, if we hope to bind God to our own limited understanding of what is best for the world, we will have cause to question whether or not He is always good and whether or not He loves us.

Young Traveler, it is essential that we remember the scope of our freedom. God created us as autonomous beings, able to enact both good and evil. The evil in the world, then, does not come from the good God who loves us, but from the broken choices of humans who have been deceived by the darkness.

It is also essential that we remember the limits of our perspectives. We cannot see as God sees, and we cannot know what is truly best for the universe. We exist within time, and God exists outside of it.

Faith, then, is the trust that God is good and that He loves us. It is what we hope for and what we choose to believe, whether we see it and understand it or not. Faith bridges the gap between logic and hope. It is essential for your journey into the field ahead.

Hope

You likely feel the despair that has crept into this forest we inhabit. In this age, there is a sense of deep hopelessness, an anguish that things are not getting better and that they will not end well. There is fear for our planet, for our physical health, for our mental wellness. There are wars and rumors of wars threatening to alter or obliterate life as we know it. There is anger, hatred, bitterness, and selfishness. These things could lead even the most virtuous to despair.

And yet, we must never forget the end of the story. We must never forget that despite the flaws and failures of humanity, the sovereign God WILL HAVE THE LAST WORD. All things shall be made whole, all things shall be made new, and those who choose to enter the Kingdom of God will experience life everlasting and glorious.

What is hope, then?

To **believe that the end of the story results in wholeness.**

As you enter the field ahead, the sense of despair that surrounds you will not lessen. Likely, dear one, it will deepen. Take care that it does not deepen in you. Hope is alive and will always be alive, and the virtue to seek it and speak it will carry you through the darkest places of your journey.

Love

There are many definitions of love, and many types of love. For our purposes here around the fire, we will speak of love as a virtue, love as the expression of God alive in us.

Here is the simplest definition of that sort of love:

To sacrifice oneself for the good of another

Jesus himself said it simply and profoundly:

John 15:13 NLT

There is no greater love than to lay down one's life for one's friends.

And just after Jesus said those words, that's exactly what He did.

The virtue of love doesn't always mean dying for those you are choosing to love. But it does mean sacrificing comfort, convenience, desire, opinion, and other sorts of things that direct our selfish wants. The virtue of love is the greatest of all the virtues; it is the culmination and expression of the best parts of every virtue. Love breaks us open and pours us out for the good of another.

The apostle Paul wrote a beautiful treatise on the virtue of love. May this guide your journey:

1 Corinthians 13:1-7 NLT

> *If I could speak all the languages of earth and of angels, but didn't love others, I would only be a noisy gong or a clanging cymbal. If I had the gift of prophecy, and if I understood all of God's secret plans and possessed all knowledge, and if I had such faith that I could move mountains, but didn't love others, I would be nothing. If I gave everything I have to the poor and even sacrificed my body, I could boast about it; but if I didn't love others, I would have gained nothing.*
>
> *Love is patient and kind. Love is not jealous or boastful or proud or rude. It does not demand its own way. It is not irritable, and it keeps no record of being wronged. It does not rejoice about injustice but rejoices whenever the truth wins out. Love never gives up, never loses faith, is always hopeful, and endures through every*

circumstance.

The Stories that You Will Tell

Pioneers, may you live a life dedicated to manifesting these virtues in the world. These virtues are the honest reflection of a human heart that has embraced the True Story. Prudence, temperance, justice, and fortitude will begin your journey toward wholeness. Faith, hope, and love alive in you will be the crowning jewels of a life becoming whole.

May the stories you tell be the stories that value virtue. May you choose to see what is real and act accordingly, to prioritize what is good in the long term over what feels good in the short term, and to advocate for each person to have the honor, dignity, provision, consequence, and rights they deserve. May you experience a determination to remain resilient and resolved to see the right thing through to the end. May you trust that God is good and that He loves us. May you choose to believe that the end of the story results in wholeness.

More than anything else, may you experience a life that is broken and poured out for the good of others. May you love well and fully, just as you are loved by your Creator.

Always remember: YOU ARE VIRTUOUS. YOU ARE A PIONEER.

Grant Me Love

If temperance be my virtue
I will think before I speak
If justice be my virtue
I will defend the weak

If fortitude be my virtue
I resolve to see things through
If prudence be my virtue
I will live by what is true

If faith be my virtue
I will trust the God of love
If hope be my virtue
I will lift my eyes above

But grant me one more virtue
To remain when others fade
Grant me love above all else
For none other I would trade

If love should by my virtue
I will see as Jesus sees
Compassion, peace, and mercy
Will flow freely out of me

If love should be my virtue
I will live as Jesus lived
By sacrifice and servanthood
With the grace to forgive

Chapter Seven

A Story of Meaning

Hope requires a surrender of your trust in the lesser things, and a trust in the greatest.

R. G. Triplett

Aria woke with a start. She had dreamt it again... the song. She lay in bed for a moment, humming the melody that played in her dreams, committing it to memory. She breathed deeply, allowing the peace and beauty of the music to enliven a peace and beauty within her.

She was going to need it.

Then she sat up and removed her outer ear blocks. She left the inner ones inside her ears, already feeling the headache coming on. The noise was *so* loud. And it never stopped. She was not ready for the onslaught of wind and rain, voice and drone, music and mayhem to overtake her senses.

Her mother had told her that it had not always been this way. Even her older sister, Bella, could remember a time before the Union took over every piece of technology on the planet. Aria had been born into this chaos – into a deafening world.

The noise started with the storms. Every day, the earth was plagued with winds and rains that drowned out the normal, peaceful quiet of the world that once was. But that was only the beginning. It was the Union that had turned the world deaf. The Union – an artificial intelligence that had taken control of the world's digital marketplace – was never silent. In fact, in a bizarre quirk of the AI, the Union could not seem to gauge the human capacity for noise, nor the human need for quiet. Perhaps because it could process limitless amounts of data, it believed that humans could process limitless amounts of noise. And so... it *blared.*

Twenty-four hours a day, every digitally connected device made noise. Advertisement after advertisement. Content piece after content piece. Work prompts, calendar reminders, media, and every sort of messaging imaginable. All at once. All the time.

The sound was deafening. Literally. Many people over the age of 50 had lost their hearing completely, and the median age for diagnosed hearing loss was dropping every year. Not to mention the rates of depression and anxiety.

Humans had adapted as best they could. Many families, like hers, disconnected all their devices at night so they could sleep. But to step outside was to enter the noise. Outside, in a world which was once enchanted by quiet, there was only chaos. They used ear blocks to help where they could, but try as they might, there seemed to be no solution to the endless noise. The digital marketplace was the marketplace of the world. To shut it down would be a global disaster.

Aria shuffled into the kitchen with a peaceful look on her face, still hearing the memories of the song in her dream.

"Were you singing in your dream again?" Bella mouthed to her.

Aria nodded and smiled.

"You must sing it for me one day," Bella said, and Aria read her lips again.

Aria shook her head. "I don't know how to sing," she replied mutely. "I'm not ready."

Bella shrugged and turned to finish her breakfast.

Aria's mother placed a hand on her shoulder, and she turned her to look at her. Her mother did not have any ear blocks, for her mother was completely deaf. She used to be a gardener.

Those with outside occupations were the youngest to lose their hearing. And yet, her mother seemed more at peace than the rest of the family. The noise could not plague her, for she had no ability to hear.

Aria looked down at the notebook her mother always carried, for she preferred to write her communication by hand.

You were born to sing. You are ready.

Aria rolled her eyes. "Thanks, mom," she said dismissively. "But I can't sing. And even if I could, no one would hear me."

Aria's mother didn't write a new response. Just tapped the notebook to encourage a second reading.

You were born to sing. You are ready.

Several weeks later, the unthinkable happened. A massive storm swept through the city and ripped the roof right off Aria's home. The storm gravely injured her mother, who had been oblivious to the deafening noise. Her father found shelter for them with the neighbors, a home with stronger walls and windows, a home with more sound dampening than most. He led the family across the street through the wind and rain, carrying Aria's mother and praying for help to come soon.

As they huddled with the neighbors in the darkness of the storm, waiting for restored power, they realized that the noise had been temporarily reduced. With no power in their immediate vicinity, there was no connection to the Union. Even as the storm raged around them, they felt a quiet settling upon their souls. They breathed into the strange peace, willing themselves to be safe. Aria's mother's eyes slipped closed, her breathing shallow.

"Aria, will you sing your song?" Bella said, and Aria could hear her words clearly this time.

"I've told you; I can't sing. I'm not ready. And what difference would it even make?" Aria felt a surge of tears press against her eyes as she gazed at her family and the neighbors.

"Please, sing us a song. Any song will do," said an older woman who lived with her neighbors. "Music can heal the deepest of wounds and calm the foulest of fears."

Aria's father put his hand on her shoulder, and then pointed her eyes towards her mother. Her bloodied hand was holding up a crumpled notebook, open to a page she had shown her daughter a hundred times before.

You were born to sing. You are ready.

Aria looked at her mother and decided she would sing for her. Even if she couldn't hear it. Even if her voice wasn't ready. Even if it didn't make any difference.

She was born to sing. She was ready.

Aria began to sing the melody that had played in her dreams for countless nights. Her voice was strong and clear. The huddled group of weary souls listened to the music and allowed their ears to take in the glorious sound of the simple song. The wind had begun to lessen as the worst of the storm has passed, and for once in their lives, they heard a singular sound cutting through every other noise in their consciousness. This was no ordinary song. This was a song that reached into the deepest parts of their soul and rekindled something that was nearly lost: *hope*.

As Aria finished her song, they all looked to her with a desperate desire for it to go on.

"Again?" Bella asked, with tears in her eyes.

And so, Aria sang again. This time, with even more confidence, more beauty, more intention. She watched the faces of the listeners, captivated and comforted, swaying to the beauty of the music, finding rest for their souls. She finished it again, and then motioned for them to join her.

The little group of survivors lifted their voices, joining in the song of hope that arose from the storm. Before long, others heard the music and came to listen, to weep, to heal, and then to sing.

Aria could hardly believe the beauty that was before her, the healing of her song.

But her mother ... her mother couldn't hear her. She longed for her mother to experience the healing for herself.

Just then, her mother raised a weak hand and pressed it against Aria's chest, feeling the vibrations in her lungs and she sang with power and strength. A smile spread across her mother's face, a smile of deep peace and contentment.

Aria continued to sing.

She was born to sing. She was ready.

The False Story:

The time has almost come for you to journey onward, but heed this last invitation well, Young Traveler. There is one more false story that we must address as we sit here by the fire. Here is the story you have been told: **The world is too far gone, and there is nothing meaningful for you to do in it.**

It is true that the world is full of noise and chaos, just like Aria and Bella experienced in the story. It is true that storms will come: the storms of circumstance, of loss, of hardship, of disaster, of brokenness, of confusion. The field ahead may prove to be a breeding ground for some of these storms, and you will experience your fair share.

And yet, to suppose that the world is too far gone, that it is beyond saving, that the noise and storms and chaos are the anthems of our age, would be to forget the story you already know. A false story which tells you that your life is meaningless is the ugliest story of them all. Let me tell you what is true.

The True Story

On the contrary, the life of a pioneer in this moment is not wiped of meaning; it is ripe with meaning. If ever there was good and important work for you to do in the world, it is now and it is here. As you step foot out of the forest and into the field, you become the bearer of a deep and essential calling, Young Traveler.

Here is the truth: **Hope is the anthem of the True Story, and you are ready to sing it.**

You see, dear one, the True Story requires an anthem. It requires a song, a refrain, a melody that will carry those who journey through its chapters to the resolution of the story. There is power in this music, power in the cadence which carries us to completion. But this anthem will only release its power when those who hear it choose to sing.

Hope is the anthem of the True Story.

Pioneers sing the song of hope.

Aria heard the song of hope, but feared she wasn't ready to sing. Feared it would not make a difference. Feared no one would hear her. And yet, when the song was most needed, she was ready. The song of hope changed everything.

We don't know the next chapters of Aria's story. Did the Union come back online? Did the storm cease? Did her mother live? Did the people start a revolution?

We don't know the next chapters, but we do know the end of the story. The end of every true story is Wholeness. Aria's song was the song of hope that would carry those characters toward their completion. And that was reason enough to sing.

The Song of the Mystic

Centuries ago, a Christian mystic lived by the name of Julian of Norwich. She lived in the Middle Ages and during the Black Death, a plague that would ravage countless English lives. She became so seriously ill that her death was imminent, and on her deathbed, she had a vision of Christ. According to her accounts, she conversed with Him in the vision. After that, she recovered from her illness and lived to write about the experience.

The words He spoke to her were many, but one line rises above all others as an anthem of hope.

> *And all shall be well.*

And all shall be well.

And all manner of things shall be well.[16]

This theme carries on repetitively through her writings as she looks upon the evils of sin, death, disease, and darkness. Repeatedly, the message from Christ is the same.

All shall be well.

All shall be well.

And all manner of things shall be well.

This is the anthem of hope. The end of the story, proclaimed in every chapter, on every page.

All shall be well.

For Such a Time as This

You may have heard of the ancient Biblical account of Queen Esther. She was a Hebrew woman who lived in the days of King Xerxes in the land of Persia. The king was searching for a new queen after his wife, Vashti, had refused to obey him. Esther was one of the maidens brought before the king for his consideration, and she quickly caught his eye. Jews in the land of Persia were outcast, so her cousin Mordecai convinced her to hide her Jewish identity. Through an incredible series of events, King Xerxes fell in love with Esther, and she became the queen.

Her cousin Mordecai was a good man, and he learned of a plot to assassinate the king. He passed the information to Esther, who related it to the king and saved his life. Trust and favor continued to build between Xerxes and Esther, and she became especially important to the king.

Meanwhile, the king's advisor, Haman, was plotting to have all the Jewish people in Persia murdered. He was furiously angry at Mordecai because Mordecai refused to bow down to Haman. He convinced the king to sign an order to kill all the Jews in the land. Mordecai pleaded with Esther to help save her people, but she responded that to approach the king without his invitation could mean her death.

Mordecai said:

> *"Don't think for a moment that because you're in the palace you will escape when all other Jews are killed. If you keep quiet at a time like this, deliverance and relief for the Jews will arise from some other place, but you and your relatives will die. Who knows if perhaps you were made queen for just such a time as this?"*
>
> *Esther 4:13-14 NLT*

Esther agreed to see the king, risking her life for the sake of the work God had called her to do.

In the end, the king's favor for Esther won him over, so he abolished the decree and sentenced Haman to die on the very gallows he had built for Mordecai.

Though this is an ancient story, the theme is altogether fitting for this moment as we sit in the forest together.

Young Traveler, I believe you were born into this world, with your particular set of skills, relationships, and dreams, for such a time as this.

It is my sincere belief that indeed you have significant, essential work to do in the world. The way you sing the anthem of hope will be different than any other human who chooses to sing it. The souls who hear your voice and witness your story may have hope kindled within them once again, and they may add their voices to sing with yours.

Consider the invitation deeply, dear one.

I believe your time is at hand.

Ready to Sing

I have told you that hope is the anthem of the True Story, and that you are ready to sing it. But how can I be sure that you are ready?

Well, of course, I cannot be sure. Only you can decide that you are ready. Although Aria's mother was convinced that she was ready to sing, it was not until Aria herself decided to sing that indeed she was ready.

What does it mean to be ready? And what does it take to be ready?

First, let us consider all the pieces of the True Story we have already talked about this night by the fire.

You are loved.

You are enchanted.

You are connected.

You are a curator.

You are becoming whole.

You are virtuous.

As you discover the truth in each of these statements, as you journey towards their embodiment in your life, you will become increasingly "ready" for all that you have been uniquely designed and created to become. The consistent practice of these realities will increase your readiness and strengthen the sound of your voice. Lean into these truths, Young Traveler, and you will soon feel the confidence within you to sing out, to join in the great anthem of all creation.

And yet … there is something more that makes you ready. Simply put, it is the Spirit of God alive in you. If you choose to receive this gift, there is a readiness that immediately prepares you to sing the song of hope.

Here's how the apostle Paul puts it:

Ephesians 2:8-9 NLT

> *God saved you by his grace when you believed. And you can't take credit for this; it is a gift from God. Salvation is not a reward for the good things we have done, so none of us can boast about it. For we are God's masterpiece. He has created us anew in Christ Jesus, so we can do the good things he planned for us long ago.*

You cannot force your own readiness. You simply receive it.

The Stories that You Will Tell

I imagine you standing on the field ahead.

Perhaps there is a battle to the west, people fighting for selfish greed and vain ambition.

Perhaps there is a party to the east, people drowning their sorrows because they have lost all sense of meaning.

Perhaps there is a storm overhead, perpetuating the noise and chaos that pretend to be the anthems of the age.

There you stand, at peace despite the chaos around you. You feel the ache of the brokenhearted who battle or numb, and yet you do not despair. You hear the noise above and you feel the ground quake below, and yet a smile plays at your lips and a confidence grips your heart.

All shall be well.

All shall be well.

And all manner of things shall be well.

You clasp hands with those around you, a circle of pioneers who have chosen to stand at your side. With courage and conviction, you lift your voices to the heavens and sing.

Always remember: YOU WERE BORN TO SING. YOU ARE READY. YOU ARE A PIONEER.

Let Me Sing

A silent song remembered
A quiet dream reborn
I'm afraid to hope
Afraid to pray
That you could use me still

A passion once forgotten
A beauty lost to fear
But whispered love
Awakens me
And shows me who I am

So Let me sing to You
Let me sing to You
A song of hope and healing
A song that You're revealing
Let me sing with You
Let me sing with You
In unforced harmony
With my Savior King
Let me sing

Your voice is growing louder
As mine fades softer now
You called my name
So I could hear
What's been there all along

The joy you offer now Lord,
Takes my breath away
I'll dare to hope
I'll take your hand
And come alive again

Let me sing out now and let your grace pour down
In a holy roar I hear your matchless sound
Let your spirit bring Your music all around
As you sing
over me

Let me sing to You
Let me sing to You
A song of hope and healing
A song that You're revealing
Let me sing with You
Let me sing with You
In unforced harmony
With my Savior King
Let me sing

Epilogue

The Field Ahead

Home is behind, the world ahead,
And there are many paths to tread
Through shadows to the edge of night,
Until the stars are all alight.

J.R.R. Tolkien

I cannot tell you precisely what you will face ahead, for I have not yet been to the field. It is our future, you see, and no one can travel to it until the current of time brings us to the threshold.

I pray my stories will guide your way, and I shall promise you this: I will go with you into this field ahead for as far as I can travel. I will cheer you on in the boundless joy of your becoming. I will run at your side until you are ready to run out ahead and lead the way.

You are not alone, and you shall never be alone, for **pioneers travel together.**

And yet I sense your trepidation, for the field ahead is not for the faint of heart.

Consider this idea, Young Traveler: in this world, you will face problems, challenges, and difficulties of many kinds. Whichever path you take from here, challenges will find you, for there is no escaping them while we live on this side of eternity.

Pioneers do not avoid problems. Pioneers simply remember that every challenge has a reason for existing.

Sometimes, you will face a challenge to show you that you have chosen the wrong path.

Sometimes, you will face a challenge to show you what you can become.

Sometimes, you will face a challenge for no other reason than to glorify God.

As you come upon these challenges, I implore you to determine which of these reasons has brought you there.

If it is because you have chosen the wrong path, do not despair. You always have a choice, and you can always forge a new path. That is the great advantage of being a pioneer.

If it is because you have an opportunity to become something more of the person you are created to be, then lean into the challenge! Rely on the virtues to see you through and celebrate your growth through the trial.

If it is for no apparent reason, then you can be sure it may still glorify God. Stand fast, look to Him, and sing the anthem of hope. All shall be well.

You are born for this moment. Your life is full of meaning, and my deepest prayer and greatest wish is that you will embrace the life you have been created to live. The God of the universe knows you by name, and He loves you with a love so powerful that it can and will overcome any darkness you will ever face. May you experience this love of God so profoundly that it overflows from you and pours out into the lives you will influence. May you choose the path through the field ahead that comes from love and leads to love, for that is the path of wholeness.

Here we stand, Young Traveler. The forest before the field.

Let us journey onward.

Pioneer of Possibility

The way ahead has not been mapped,
For none have gone before me.
I cannot follow trails or tracks,
No, this is a new story.

This crossroads begs no turning back;
Ahead is all I know.
And yet without a guide or map,
Wherever shall I go?

To climb a mountain yet unseen,
Or ford river wide,
Or sail across an unknown sea
Will take more than my pride.

I must learn how to blaze a trail,
Since others long to come.
A guiding light might still prevail,
So steady, I go on.

No roads, no maps, no trails or tracks
And yet, perhaps one tool
A compass may yet guide my path
And lead me by its rule.

The One True North will call to me
When darkness clouds my view.
With time and care I'll learn to see
And find the best way through.

Into the woods I go at last,
The country undiscovered.
The future pulls me from the past

And I will travel onward.

The ancient ways will cast out fear,
And then I'll be set free.
I find myself a pioneer
Of possibility.

For Further Reading

This field guide contains only the briefest glimpses into some of the great storytellers and thinkers. This list will provide you with some resources to further your journey.

Books of stories:

The Chronicles of Narnia by C.S. Lewis

The Hobbit by J.R.R. Tolkien

The Lord of the Rings Trilogy by J.R.R. Tolkien

The Wingfeather Saga by Andrew Peterson

The Epic of Haven Trilogy by R.G. Triplett

The Harry Potter Series by J.K. Rowling

Prince Warrior Series by Priscilla Shirer

The Circle Series by Ted Dekker

Once Upon a Wardrobe by Patti Callahan

The Cooper Kids Adventure Series by Frank Peretti

Hidden Figures by Margot Le Shetterly

When Stars are Scattered by Victoria Jamieson and Omar Mohamed

The Lost Year by Katherine Marsh

Hoot by Carl Hiaasen

Books of wisdom:

The Wisdom Pyramid by Brett McCracken

Daily Disciplines by Skip Ross

Everybody, Always by Bob Goff

Soundtracks by John Acuff

Do Hard Things by Alex and Brett Harris

Now I See by Zach Elliott

The Artisan Soul by Erwin McManus

The 7 Habits of Highly Effective People by Steven Covey

Just Courage by Gary A. Haugen

One Thousand Gifts by Ann Voskamp

Atomic Habits by James Clear

All It Takes is a Goal by John Acuff

Hero on a Mission by Donald Miller

Discussion Guide

Here are some questions to guide conversations about the stories and truths shared in the pages of this field guide. Remember, pioneers travel together. These questions will give you opportunity to give and receive insight among those who choose to journey with you.

CHAPTER ONE: **A Story of Love**

1. Have you ever felt confused about your place in the world, like the princess? Where did you look to find a place to belong?

2. Have you ever had someone tell you lies about who you are? If so, what strategies did you use to remember the truth about who you are?

3. What does it mean to be loved?

4. How do you experience the love of God in your life?

5. What does being beloved by the Creator mean to you?

6. What is a practical way you can become love to those

around you?

7. How does the poem about the dancer make you feel? What connections can you make between the princess and the dancer?

CHAPTER TWO: **A Story of Enchantment**

1. How can you relate to the boy in the story?

2. In what ways have you perceived the magic of the light in the world?

3. In what ways have you perceived the magic of the darkness in the world?

4. In what ways have you perceived magic within you?

5. Can you share a story about how your words had more power than you expected?

6. What sort of things do you believe God wants to create with you?

7. What is a practical way you can bring hope and healing to those around you?

CHAPTER THREE: **A Story of Connection**

1. Have you ever felt like the baker in the story?

2. Have you ever felt like your contributions didn't matter to someone? How did that make you feel?

3. Has someone ever loved you by listening to you?

4. How does being silent in order to listen and understand make you feel?

5. What is a practical way you can express empathy for someone?

6. Tell us about a time when you collaborated with someone. How did it go? How did you feel when you accomplished a goal together?

7. How have you seen comparison or competition affect those around you?

8. What are some practical ways you can cultivate connection in your life?

CHAPTER FOUR: A Story of Stewardship

1. Have you ever felt like the man in the story, with your environment out of control? How did that make you feel?

2. What are some ways you can experience, steward, or curate the beauty of God's creation?

3. What are you currently a steward of? How does stewarding these things make you feel?

4. What are some practical ways you can steward something entrusted to your care?

5. What are some practical ways you can curate goodness, truth, and beauty in your life?

6. Read the verse below from the chapter:

   Philippians 4:8-9 NLT

   And now, dear brothers and sisters, one final thing. Fix your thoughts on what is true, and honorable, and right, and pure, and lovely, and admirable. Think about things that are excellent and worthy of praise. Keep putting into practice all you learned and received from me—everything you heard from me and saw me doing. Then the God of peace will be with you.

   What practices or habits have you put in place to fix your thoughts on what is true, honorable, right, pure, lovely or admirable?

CHAPTER FIVE: **A Story of Wholeness**

1. Which creature in the story do you most relate to?

Why?

2. Which area of life do you feel strongest in? Which area of life do you feel weakest in?

3. What are some ways you can affirm and achieve when it comes to your physical health?

   What about when it comes to your mental health??

   Your social health?

   Your spiritual health?

4. What are some healthy habits you would like to build into your life?

5. What makes you feel fully alive and flourishing, like the lamb in the story?

6. Who is a person in your life who reminds you of the lamb in the story? Why?

CHAPTER SIX: **A Story of Virtue**

1. Which character in the story do you most relate to? Why?

2. How can you choose what is real and act accordingly in your daily life?

3. How can you practice resilience in your daily life?

4. The four cardinal virtues are:

   - Prudence
   - Temperance
   - Justice
   - Fortitude

   How do you see yourself displaying one of these virtues? How could you grow in that area?

1. The three Christian virtues are:

   - Faith
   - Hope
   - Love

   How do you see yourself displaying one of these virtues? How could you grow in that area?

CHAPTER SEVEN: **A Story of Meaning**

1. What are the noisy things in your life that get in the way of you hearing the song of hope?

2. What does hope mean to you?

3. What do you hope for?

4. How can you practically lean into the truths that:

   You are loved.

   You are enchanted.

   You are connected.

   You are a curator.

   You are becoming whole.

   You are virtuous.

   You are ready.

5. How does it make you feel to know that you were born for such a time as this, placed in this world right where you are by a loving Creator for a particular reason?

6. Do you feel ready to sing? If so, how? If not, what can this group of pioneers do to help you move toward readiness?

A Final Invitation

As you look to the field ahead, Young Traveler, I want to invite you to join a community of pioneers who are on this journey of becoming with you. We are learning the truths written in this Field Guide together, day by day, week by week, month by month, and year by year. I invite you to walk alongside others who, like you, have sat by the fire and heard the stories about embracing their role as pioneers. I invite you to share your own stories with fellow travelers who might learn from your experience and wisdom. I invite you to hear the tales and triumphs of those who have gone before you. Pioneers travel together, and you are welcomed into a community where we are continually working to resource you for the journey ahead.

There are three ways you can join this community of pioneers.

First, we invite you to **connect with us online**. Visit our website, www.pioneercircle.org, to learn more and discover some free resources to guide you onward. You can follow our social media here:

Instagram:

@PioneerCircle

@CircleAinsta

Threads:

@PioneerCircle

@CircleAinsta

Facebook:

Pioneer Circle

Circle A

Secondly, we invite you to **become a part of the Pioneer Circle!** This is a community of monthly subscribers who pioneer together. You will connect with incredible leaders who will come alongside you to champion your progress and to equip you to navigate the undiscovered spaces in the field ahead. As a part of this community of pioneers, you will receive access to our goal setting app, weekly video content, monthly coaching calls, group challenges, and personal encouragement as you grow to be a pioneer of possibility. It would be an honor and privilege to walk alongside you through the Pioneer Circle!

You can find more information about how to join the Pioneer Circle here: www.pioneercircle.org.

Finally, we invite you to **join us at the Circle A Summit**. This immersive camp experience will expand on the topics of this book as we provide resources and community to help you learn, connect, and grow. More than that, the Summit will give you the opportunity to invest personal time with those on this journey with you, and with those who have traveled before you. The best part is that the Summit takes place in at atmosphere of adventure and joy, where you will get to participate in all sorts of exhilarating and entertaining experiences! The aim of The Circle A Summit is to create a nurturing space for the Circle of God's Agape love, where everyone is embraced, included, and respected. Within this environment, we hold the belief that we can become all that God created us to be.

You can find more information about how to participate in the Circle A Summit here: www.circleacamp.com

Afterword

What makes truth *sticky*? You know ... where it becomes not just something we remember, but something we become? The most impactful searches for truth are less about the fact or the lesson or even the answer we were looking for, and more about forming a new way of thinking altogether.

If you look at the history of human civilization, from our earliest written accounts, you will find one thing we have undeniably in common, regardless of culture or time period.

We tell stories.

Stories matter, and stories last. Stories have a relentless tenacity to hang around in our memories and mental pathways, to stick in our thoughts in such a way that it is nearly impossible to wholly forget them.

Now, I can almost guarantee that you would be hard-pressed to recite the innumerable lists of facts and dates and formulas that each of us were required to memorize while we were in school. But if I asked you to recount an event, or share with me a memory, or tell me something important that you learned over the years in school, you would most certainly be able to tell me a story.

Think of all the fables, the Bible stories, the mythologies, and the parables that we read and sing about. Our poems and playground chants, our urban legends and cautionary tales; all of them stick with us for a reason.

Truth becomes so much stickier when it is found within the framework of a struggle, a triumph, a defeat; in a story of both the folly and the fortitude of the human spirit. I would argue that stories remind us that our flourishing is less about explaining and quantifying the truth and more about understanding ourselves in light of it.

I hope that you found yourself in the stories of this guide. I sincerely pray that the truths woven all throughout these pages will start to get sticky for you, too.

And hey... when you find yourself in a spot that feels like the stories of the Pioneers in these pages, perhaps you will be reminded of the wisdom to go back and reread and remember these stories all over again. You never know what new kind of truths you might discover.

Seek the Light,

R. G. Triplett

Acknowledgements

This book was born out of a movement of pioneers. It is a privilege and an honor to offer thanks to the individuals and communities who have helped bring these stories to life.

To my daughters, **Brenna and Kayla Farrell**: These stories are for you, given as just a glimpse of many more stories we will tell together. As you travel into the field ahead, may you be assured of the love and legacy that will always accompany you in every moment of your journey. I am so proud of you and the incredible young women you are becoming. I cannot wait to witness the stories your lives will tell.

To my parents, **Skip and Susan Ross**: You changed the lives of generations of young people with your stories, your love, your generosity, and your example. Every page of this book contains your fingerprints, and every person who reads it will receive the legacy of your love. Thank you for living the stories you taught and for teaching the stories you lived. Thank you for Circle A. We will continue to Pass it On.

To my husband, **Chris Farrell**: I am so grateful for the past 20 years of creating art and beauty with you. What a gift it is that our work, ministry, passions, and family can all combine into one amazing adventure of a life. You are always my biggest support and steadfast rock. Thank you for helping me rest, celebrate, laugh, and grow along the journey.

To my coach, **Zach Elliott**: This book would not exist without you. Thank you for being a source of strength and encouragement. Thank you for your imagination, wisdom, and guidance. Thank you for championing the life and beauty of the gospel in the world and for inviting me to be a part of the adventure. I can't wait to see what is next!

To my editing team, **Benjamin NeSmith, Yvonne Farrell, and Darah Woomert:** Your tender care of the words on these pages cannot be overstated. Thank you, from the bottom of my heart, for taking the risk and giving the time to edit these pages into something better than they were when they started. You have stewarded more than these words; you have stewarded the hope of what these words can mean in the world, and you have stewarded my heart in the process. I am beyond grateful.

To my dear friend and Circle A Summit Assistant Director, **Danielle Dorey**: Thank you for the endless encouragement and support you have given to the mission of Circle A and the Pioneer Circle. Thank you for the care and wisdom you poured into me through the process of writing this book. Your help in the final stages of writing helped to birth this project from a manuscript to a finished book, and I am forever grateful for your time and talents. Thank you for seeing this thing through to the end!

To my sister-in-law and artist, **Amanda Farrell**: The hand-crafted love and beauty you gave to this project has brought it to life! Thank you for sharing your skill to create this imagery. I pray thousands of young imaginations will be welcomed into these stories because of your efforts and talents.

To my friend and graphic designer, **Rob Stainback**: Your work has laid a foundation of excellence and beauty for every title we have released as Lost Poet Press. Thank you for sticking with me all these years and for bringing your talents to our projects. They are always better because of you.

To my Lost Poet partner, **R. G. Triplett**: I never could have known what adventures awaited us as we offered the poets a place to call home. Thank you for trusting me and believing in me. Thank you for allowing me to steward your stories and thank you for tending to mine. You are a Warrior Poet, and I am honored to fight at your side for the hope of the world.

To my church family, **Element Church**: You have taught me what strength, faithfulness, grace, humility, and integrity are. It has been my joy and honor to worship on the mountain with you. Another story wouldn't do. Thank you for all the ways you have joined in the journey of this project. Thank you for seeking to uncover the mystery of God's love for all creation, and for embodying the hope and healing of Jesus. Thank you for learning together what it means to nurture lives of adoration, formation, and love. We will all share in celebration at the feast, my Beloved friends.

To my mentor group, **Team Canvas**: It is not every day that a team of heroes, mentors, and champions welcomes you into their intimate space of community. To be not only welcomed but respected among you has been such an encouragement to my heart and a major source of energy for the rebirth of Circle A. Thank you for all the ways you have partnered, supported, given, led, and loved through this process. May God bless you in your faithfulness.

To my **Circle A Community** of Summit attendees, Pioneer Circle Members, Reflections Cast listeners, and generations of Circle A family: The field awaits us ahead. Let us be bold! Let us be brave! Let us journey forward together as pioneers into a Great Adventure!

Endnotes

1 Lewis, C. S. **The Chronicles of Narnia**. New York: Harper Collins, First American Edition, 2001, p. 141

2 Lewis, C. S. **Mere Christianity**. Touchstone, First Touchstone edition, 1996, p. 121.

3 Lewis, C. S. **The Chronicles of Narnia**. New York: Harper Collins, First American Edition, 2001, p. 633.

4 **The Lord of the Rings: The Fellowship of the Ring**. Directed by Peter Jackson, Performance by Elijah Wood, Ian McKellen, Liv Tyler, Viggo Mortensen, Sean Astin, and Cate Blanchett, New Line Cinema, 2001.

5 Rowling, J. K. **"Harry Potter and the Deathly Hallows: Part 2".** Dir. David Yates. Perf. Daniel Radcliffe, Emma Watson, and Rupert Grint. Warner Bros. Pictures, 2011. DVD.

6 The phrasing of this false story is based on the work of Friedrich Nietzsche.

7 Tolkien, J.R.R. **The Fellowship of the Ring**. Houghton Mifflin, 1988, pp. 155-156.

8 **Encanto**. Directed by Jared Bush, Byron Howard, Charise Castro Smith. With Stephanie Beatriz, María Cecilia Botero, John Leguizamo, Mauro Castillo. Walt Disney Pictures; Walt Disney Animation Studios. 2021.

9 Covey, Stephen R. **The Seven Habits of Highly Effective People**. Free Press Trade Paperback Edition, Simon and Schuster, 2004, p. 235

10 Lee, Harper. **To Kill a Mockingbird**. First Perennial Classic edition, Harper Press, 2002, p. 33.

11 Seuss, Dr. **The Lorax**. New York, Random House, 1999, p. 59.

12 Buechner, Frederick. https://www.frederickbuechner.com/quote-of-the-day/2017/11/17/the-kingdom

13 This parable is recorded by Xenophon in ***Memorabilia*** 2.1.21–34.

14 Covey, Stephen R. **The Seven Habits of Highly Effective People**: 30th Anniversary Edition, Simon and Schuster, 4th edition, 2020, kindle.

15 Lewis, C. S. **The Screwtape Letters**. HarperOne, First Harper Collins Hardback Edition, 2001, p. 161.

16 Julian of Norwich. **Revelations of Divine Love**. 1412, first published 1901, Amazon Kindle edition, p. 54.

References

Prologue

Frost, Robert. "Stopping by Woods on a Snowy Evening" from **The Poetry of Robert Frost**, edited by Edward Connery Lathem. Henry Holt and Company, 1923, 1969.

Chapter One

DiCamillo, Kate. **The Tale of Despereaux: Being the Story of a Mouse, a Princess, Some Soup, and a Spool of Thread**. Candlewick Press, 2006, p. 81.

Chapter Two

Lewis, C. S. **The Weight of Glory.** HarperOne, 2001, p. 46.

Chapter Three

Peterson, Andrew. "Carry the Fire". **Light for the Lost Boy**, Centricity Music, 2012.

Chapter Four

Berry, Wendell. **A Timbered Choir: The Sabbath Poems 1979-1997**. Counterpoint, 1998, p. 209.

Chapter Five

O'Donohue, John. **To Bless the Space Between Us**. "For Solitude",

Convergent Press, 2008, p. 112.

Chapter Six

Dickens, Charles. **David Copperfield**. Amazon Kindle, 2023, p. 164.

Chapter Seven

Triplett, R.G. **The Great Darkening.** Lost Poet Press, First Hardcover Edition, 2014, p. 369.

Epilogue

Tolkien, J.R.R. **The Fellowship of the Ring**. Houghton Mifflin, 1988, p. 87.

Printed in the USA
CPSIA information can be obtained
at www.ICGtesting.com
CBHW071214280624
10823CB00042B/934